WHEN THE MAN IN YOUR LIFE CAN'T COMMIT

Dr. David Hawkins

HARVEST HOUSE PUBLISHERS

EUGENE, OREGON

Cover by Koechel Peterson & Associates, Minneapolis, Minnesota

This book includes stories in which the author has changed people's names and some details of their situations to protect their privacy.

WHEN THE MAN IN YOUR LIFE CAN'T COMMIT
Copyright © 2006 by David Hawkins
Published by Harvest House Publishers
Eugene, Oregon 97402
www.harvesthousepublishers.com

Library of Congress Cataloging-in-Publication Data
  Hawkins, David, 1951-
    When the man in your life can't commit / David Hawkins.
        p. cm.
    Includes bibliographical references.
    ISBN-13: 978-0-7369-1650-9 (pbk.)
    ISBN-10: 0-7369-1650-4
1. Commitment (Psychology)—Religious aspects—Christianity. 2. Man-woman relationships—Religious aspects—Christianity. 3. Marriage—Religious aspects—Christianity. 4. Sex role—Religious aspects—Christianity. 5. Men (Christian theology) I. Title.
    BV4597.53.C56H39 2006
    248.8'4—dc22   2005023013

Printed in the United States of America

      06   07   08   09   10   11   12   / DP-CF /   10   9   8   7   6   5   4   3   2   1

*This book is gratefully dedicated
to the countless women
who wait for their Prince Charming,
their knight in shining armor.
Never, never settle for less.*

Acknowledgments

The book began when the fabulous sales and marketing team at Harvest House Publishers suggested the need for a book about commitment. They entrusted me with the project. For that, and for them, I am thankful. I know they have worked to prepare for the publication of this book and will continue working to bring the book to the marketplace. I have come to deeply appreciate every one of them and their immense talents. I think the world of that bunch of fun, dynamic, and creative people.

I owe a special word of thanks to Terry Glaspey, who has, from my beginning at Harvest House, encouraged me to write what is on my heart. Terry, you challenged me in the beginning of this book in ways that made the book better. I get to write for a wonderful publishing house and am supported in that endeavor. Thank you. I won't let you down.

Another word of thanks goes to Gene Skinner. Gene, you know the tireless work you do for me. I feel as if you have become my own personal editor. Not that I am always thrilled to subject my writing to your scrutiny, but I have come to trust that you will always make my writing clearer and sharper. I am thankful to have you on my team. Let's do another one together!

I am also indebted to Jim Lemonds. Jim, your critique of my writing always makes it better. You boldly tell me when things just don't flow or when my personal pronouns are out of whack. I'm always cautious to hear what you have to say. Your words are filled with the wisdom of a seasoned writer.

My special thanks go to my fiancée, Christie. Christie, my relationship with you was the catalyst for some of the writing in this book. I found myself surprisingly in the middle of some personal stuff even as I was imparting truths to my readers. As I challenged my readers, I challenged myself. I suppose that is the way it should be, and hopefully it made my writing even more fresh and alive. You helped me live out my truths. Thanks, Sweetie.

I can't thank my wonderful parents enough for the stable and loving Christian home in which I was raised. You remind of the powerful truths of Scripture, especially Jeremiah 29:11. Thanks, Mom and Dad!

As always, I thank the Lord for the opportunity to write. I am always amazed that I am allowed to pursue my passion of writing. I am a blessed man—sitting in my loft writing studio, overlooking Puget Sound, soaking up God's greatness.

CONTENTS

Prologue:
A Healing Journey
to Healthy Commitment

And they will become one flesh.

GENESIS 2:24

Can you remember the feeling of liking a boy more than he liked you? Feeling the heartache while waiting in the deafening silence for the phone to ring? Fidgety and irritable, knowing your affections would not be returned—at least not with the same intensity. Nothing is worse.

You were ready for a relationship; he balked. You had the wedding planned, the babies named, and the house decorated; he was thinking about making the baseball team.

Now, as an adult, you find yourself with similar feelings, similar problems. You are ready to write him into the story of your future but find yourself wondering if his story has the same ending. You are committed to him, but is he as committed to you? Are you as central to his life as he is to yours? Rejection still stings.

These thorny dilemmas are the focus of this book. We will address the most likely reasons he won't commit, the natural stages of commitment, and how your own issues with commitment muddy the waters. We will talk about how you can help him get ready for a lasting, loving, and intimate relationship.

One balmy evening, when the moon was hanging low in the sky like a beckoning light for meandering boys, I had just started to slip into a peaceful sleep when I heard the familiar tap-tap-tap on my window.

"Hey," Kenny whispered. "Are you coming with us? Are you in?"

Half-dazed, I took a moment to remember the plans we had made earlier in the day.

It had all seemed simple, exciting, and adventurous when the four of us boys lay in the afternoon sun and discussed our evening escapade. Now I felt a hazy tinge of fear.

Kenny's words settled into my ears.

"Are you in?"

I peered out into the moonlit night and saw Mike and Donald hovering nearby. Obviously, they were "in."

Would I be in? Would I open the window, crawl through the small opening, and slip away without awakening my parents, whose bedroom was upstairs directly above mine?

The adrenaline began to pulse through my body. We would be soldiers maneuvering into hostile territory—on a mission to escape the confines of our bedrooms and our parents' control, to stealthily work our way to the golf course to spy on golfers using the well-lit driving range a few blocks away, before returning to base without being noticed.

But was I "in"?

I was paralyzed by the weight of a decision I had thought would be so simple. Moments passed like hours before Kenny tapped again on the window, scrunching his face against the pane. He was growing impatient.

"Come on! We have to get going."

What would I do? Here was one of my first requests to make a commitment.

Fast-forward four years. As an awkward 15-year-old, nervous and incredibly self-conscious, I was again faced with the question, "Are you in?" And once again, I found myself paralyzed.

This time I was trying to answer that harrowing adolescent question: "Will you go steady with me?" I was trying to work up the courage to write a girl into my future. And I balked.

Karen was a cute brunette I'd become acquainted with at our church youth group. Actually, I had known her for several years, but suddenly, as a result of that strange phenomenon called *puberty*, she looked far more attractive. We had engaged in the typical dance: Boy eyes girl and girl eyes boy; boy and girl engage in uncomfortable small talk.

Sort of.

In truth, I had my friends talk to her friends to see if she might be interested in me. Word trickled back that indeed she was. Now what? It took me a few days—all right, I suppose it was a few weeks—to decide on my next move. But while I was making up my mind, Karen was changing hers.

I was stunned to learn she was no longer interested in me because of my failure to make a commitment. I had waited too long. My hesitance showed that I was afraid, and she wanted no part of that. She was looking for someone who wanted to be with her and was willing to say so.

To a sensitive adolescent heart, this was devastating. It would be my first, though certainly not my last, romantic rejection. All because I couldn't decide. All because I wouldn't commit. All because I failed to share my fumbling emotions with her.

As the years passed I continued to grapple with commitment and emotional vulnerability. I have gradually become aware of my struggle with being committed and emotionally available in relationships. This has become a measuring stick for how my relationships are functioning.

At times, things have come easily, but too often they have been incredibly difficult. I've learned that the more I am able to be fully present in my relationships, the more gratifying they are. The more I am willing to dedicate myself to them, the more intimacy becomes available to me. The more I am willing to share my truest heart, the more warmth and attachment I enjoy.

In the many years that have passed since that youthful evening, I have come to realize that making choices is a part of everyday life. In our relationships, we are constantly confronted with the same decisions: Will we commit ourselves to those we care about? Will we write them into the future of our lives? Will we risk letting them know us intimately? Sneaking out a bedroom window at midnight is child's play, of course. Committing ourselves to another for life is something with much greater ramifications.

Why the Concern?

Of course, I'm not the only one grappling with commitment and intimacy. In one form or another, these issues are on everyone's mind. Who does not wrestle with their man being uncommitted, unemotional, or insensitive? As a woman you are looking for a committed relationship with a man who is willing to be emotionally vulnerable. You want a man who is willing to put his emotions on the table and talk straight from the heart. You want a caring companion, not an overworked, insulated robot. You want emotional availability and an intense interest in *you!* You want him to risk as much as you do—preparing to make a lifelong attachment to you.

But therein lies the problem. What you want is no trivial matter. To many men, you are asking for the moon. You want him to foreclose on all other options to seek happiness with just you. Too many men smirk at the suggestion. You want a man to share the hidden recesses of his heart with you? Too many men don't know what lurks in those dark places and are ill-equipped to explore them on their own, let alone with you.

The challenge is daunting. You may be tempted to settle into a subtle but niggling cynicism. Is trying to build mutual commitment really worth the trouble? Are any men willing to put it out there for you? Is it worth reading a book to learn more about this complex issue? Yes. Not only is it worth it, but you can learn more about the problem and become more skilled at determining whether your man has the goods to be committed to you. You can learn how to make better choices in relationships. You can learn if you have the goods to be a committed and emotionally vulnerable woman.

I suspect we agree that many people struggle with commitment. We might even agree that concern over emotional vulnerability is worthy of our consideration. But a book on the topic? Is that not a bit much? In a word—*no!* We have not talked enough about the importance of commitment and its impact on relationships. Likewise, we have not learned nearly enough about the significance of emotional vulnerability.

Many people, especially men, remain underdeveloped emotionally, afraid of sharing their innermost thoughts and emotions. Many are tentative, unwilling to jump into a committed relationship with both feet. This hesitancy, these fears of commitment, cause havoc in marriage and other relationships. That is why talking about these issues in a straightforward manner is so important.

In nearly 30 years of counseling, I have seen few men who know what they feel, think, and want, and who are willing to share those feelings, thoughts, and desires with their partner. You know the dire statistics as well as I do—more than 50 percent of first marriages fail; an even greater percentage of second marriages disintegrate. That's why I suggest we need to revisit this topic of commitment, attachment, and emotional vulnerability with new fervor. We need to learn anew what constitutes commitment and how to overcome the barriers to it. We need to examine strategies for creating real intimacy with your man and overcoming the obstacles that stand in the way. As we tackle these issues, we will enjoy the beauty of enduring relationship as God intended it.

Struggles with intimacy, of course, are not limited to our contact with one another—many of us are challenged to feel a vibrant contact with God as well. As we wrestle with creating a safe and caring relationship with our mate, we also seem to waver in our commitment and intimacy with God. We say that we desire intimacy with God and yet complain that we cannot hear His voice. We quickly forget the importance of Jesus' words: "I am the vine, you are the branches. If a man remains in me and I in him, he will bear much fruit; apart from me you can do nothing" (John 15:5). How can we learn to commit ourselves to our mate, to one another, and to God? What does your relationship with God have to do with true contact with your man?

Working Definitions

Before going any further, perhaps we should agree on working definitions for *commitment* and *emotional vulnerability*, the central issues of the book.

You may recognize the message about commitment in these lines from Paul Reiser's book *Couplehood*. Reiser, in typical male fashion, says that while preparing to discuss the issue of relational commitment and suitability for one another, he had the following conversation with his potential mate.

> "I snore."
> "That's okay."
> "No, but I snore in odd, little rhythms."
> "Doesn't bother me."
> "I once snored a medley from *The King and I.*"
> "My favorite musical."
> "All right…I just thought you should know."

"And you keep raising the ante," Reiser tells us. "Not that you want to scare them off; it's just that if they're ever going to leave you, let's get it out of the way now."

> "You may notice that in the bathroom, I tend to flush a few seconds before I'm actually done. I don't know why, I just do. And there's no way I can change. Do you understand this? Can you accept this? Because it has cost me dearly in the past."

Reiser adds this hopeful comment: "And she still hasn't changed her mind."[1]

Reiser's story is humorous, and on the surface he is questioning the commitment level of his partner. One cannot help but wonder, however, about his commitment level. Is he truly testing his partner for her level of commitment, or is he making it clear that he is only "in" on his terms? Is he telling her that she must be aware that he has no intention of changing and may be, in fact, putting her on notice that he has one foot out the door? His commitment level is suspect at best.

Taking Reiser at face value, we might define commitment as *knowing all of your partner's idiosyncrasies and still choosing to stay with him*. It is *a dedication to, over time, understand and accept the foibles of your mate*. This definition is at least partly true, but it is not enough. We do need to know what we're in for and whether we can take it when the real person comes out to play. But commitment is far more than this.

One of the simplest and most profound working definitions of commitment I've heard came from my editor, Terry Glaspey, who said that commitment means *writing our loved ones into our personal future*. They become part and parcel of a life that extends far beyond the present.

No question about it. When we think about where we will be in the future, our mate should be there beside us. When we make plans for the months and years to come, we must take the well-being of our mate into account. When we consider the inevitable losses we will encounter, we can take refuge in knowing that our mate will be there to share the struggles. And as we anticipate the joys that will come our way, the celebrant closest to us will be our mate.

Scott Peck, in his landmark book *The Road Less Traveled*, adds to this working definition of commitment. In a section titled "The Risk of Commitment," he says commitment is the foundation and bedrock of any genuinely loving relationship. "Couples cannot resolve in any healthy way the universal issues of marriage—dependency and independency, dominance and submission, freedom and fidelity, for example—without the security of knowing that the act of struggling over these issues will not itself destroy the relationship."[2]

If this is the heart of commitment, what do we mean by *emotional vulnerability?* Emotional vulnerability is intimacy, or *into-me-see.* It means *revealing our truest self, including our deepest thoughts, values, and feelings, to another.* When we are emotionally vulnerable, we risk sharing uncomfortable thoughts and feelings. We reveal aspects of ourselves that we might share with no one else. Because intimacy demands intensely personal sharing, it becomes sacred. It is a place you share with your mate and God.

Another descriptor of emotional vulnerability is *being real.* You may be familiar with the famous story by Margery Williams in which a toy rabbit learns the lessons and risks of being real.

> "Does it hurt?" asked the Rabbit.
>
> "Sometimes," said the Skin Horse, for he was always truthful. "When you are Real you don't mind being hurt."
>
> "Does it happen all at once, like being wound up," he asked, "or bit by bit?"
>
> "It doesn't happen all at once," said the Skin Horse. "You become. It takes a long time. That's why it doesn't often happen to people who break easily, or have sharp

edges, or who have to carefully be kept. Generally, by the time you are Real, most of your hair has been loved off, and your eyes drop out and you get loose in the joints and very shabby. But these things don't matter at all, because once you are Real you can't be ugly, except to people who don't understand."

The Rabbit sighed. He thought it would be a long time before this magic called Real happened to him. He longed to become Real, to know what it felt like: and yet the idea of growing shabby and losing his eyes and whiskers was rather sad. He wished that he could become it without these uncomfortable things happening to him."[3]

Ah, how I relate to Rabbit! I want closeness without pain. I want the strokes without losing anything in the process. I want guarantees, assurances that whatever love I offer will come back to me manifold.

I surely don't want to lose my eyes and hair, so to speak, in the process of being cared about for who I am! But Skin Horse knows. Skin Horse understands that we must pay a price if we want to experience the joys of being Real. And it is worth the price. In this book, we will learn more about that process—the process of achieving emotional vulnerability within commitment. You will learn what makes a man tick and what he will need to emotionally commit himself to you and your relationship.

Commitment Is Crucial

A relationship without commitment is barren. It is the shell of the house without the inner furnishings; a house but not a home.

Cindy knew this all too personally. A modestly built, vivacious 30-year-old, she carried herself with an air of confidence that came from years of work as a travel agent. She had a broad, generous smile that belied her anxiety. Beneath her professional expertise and assurance lay hidden fears.

Cindy quickly shared in counseling that she had enjoyed several wonderful relationships over the past few years, but each one stopped short of the altar. She now found herself confused and profoundly discouraged. She wondered if she was doing something wrong.

She came to counseling because her current relationship appeared headed in the same discouraging, dead-end direction. She shared that she had not wanted anything too serious in her early twenties, but now, as a 30-year-old, things were different. Relationships were becoming more important. She wanted solidity, stability, and children. She wanted a secure future with a man. *Was this too much to ask for?* she wondered.

"I used to assume that the right man would come along in due time, and things would be fine. I didn't take relationships seriously a few years ago. Then I sensed that the clock was ticking, and I want children. So, I started to open myself up to the possibility of something more serious. I became ready for a committed relationship, and I know that's crucial to a lasting marriage. But nothing has worked out for me. Men don't seem willing to commit. I'm not sure what the problem is."

Cindy began to cry as she reached for the tissue box.

"I'm wondering now if it's something about me. The first time a man walked out on me, it hurt, but I assumed it was something about him. The second time a guy wouldn't commit, it hurt worse. I want things to work out with Todd, my boyfriend, but it doesn't look too promising."

"Tell me about Todd," I said.

Cindy shared that Todd was a handsome man, a rugged 34-year-old divorcé who owned his own contracting firm. He was a Christian man she met a year ago in their singles group at church. He had shared how happy he was with her. He and Cindy had many things in common, including a desire for children, and they had grown steadily closer in their dating relationship. They both loved the outdoors, and Cindy was surprised and delighted by his willingness to watch movies and attend the theater with her. They shared similar spiritual values, enjoyed church activities, and even prayed together. They laughed easily and often. Cindy believed that she had found her soul mate. She loved him, and he loved her.

All the ingredients were in place for a wonderful future together. She was poised for the next, and crucial final step—commitment. But that's where the good news ended.

Cindy again paused in sharing her story. She appeared puzzled, apparently still trying to understand why the natural progression would stop. Why would such beautiful music become muted?

"When we start talking about our future, he gets tongue-tied. He says that it's time, but our conversations are stifled whenever he tries to pose the big question. He says he must not be ready, but he's been saying that now for six months. Then he adds that he can't give me any promises, that he just doesn't know what the future will hold. I am so frustrated and hurt."

Cindy clearly still winced in pain from earlier rejections as well as the distancing maneuvers by Todd. She was saddened to think this serious relationship might end the way the others had—with her feeling rejected, her self-esteem wounded.

"I love Todd. He's right for me, and I think I'm right for him. I just don't know if he's ready to make a lifelong commitment to me. I take commitment very seriously, and I just don't know if he is ready. But I've been through this before. Am I expecting too much? Should I just hang in there and give him more time? What's wrong with me, Doctor Hawkins?"

I reassured Cindy that her feelings were normal and under-standable. I affirmed that her desire for commitment was a healthy thing. Relationships should not be like railroad tracks heading off into the distance—parallel lives that never come together or go anyplace in particular. God created us for intimacy and commitment. We need both in order to feel complete and whole.

Jan's story was a bit different. She had been married to Tom for 20 years and, at least on the surface, felt that he was committed to her. Yet she had not felt particularly close to him for most of their marriage.

As this couple sat in front of me, I could see the pain in their faces.

"What's the problem?" I asked, noticing the tears in Jan's eyes. Tom stared silently at her.

"I am just so discouraged," Jan said, dabbing at her eyes. "No matter how many times I tell him, Tom still doesn't know how to share his feelings with me or own up to his problems. He still blames everyone else for things, and it drives me crazy. Just last night we had a huge fight over another broken promise. He told me we'd have a date Saturday night, but he chose to help out a buddy instead. It all boils down to him hurting me again and again and then wondering why I don't want to be intimate with him."

I watched as Tom bristled at her words.

"There just doesn't seem to be anything I can do to make her happy," he blurted. "She makes me out to be some kind of monster, and I'm not. I'm just as frustrated as she is. We haven't had sex in two months. How do you think I feel about that?"

"But Tom, can you see how Jan needs you to be committed to emotional intimacy before there can be sexual intimacy?" I asked.

"I suppose," he offered grudgingly. "But I'm trying."

Jan looked away, obviously exasperated.

"What are you feeling, Jan?" I asked.

"Well, this may seem harsh, but I don't think he is committed to me. Not to really being with me and meeting my needs. If he were, he'd make more of an effort to do some of the simple things I ask for. I don't ask for that much."

I sensed their overwhelming frustration and hopelessness. They had been working on these issues for several months and still seemed no closer to having an intimate relationship where they could safely be emotionally vulnerable with one another. They had the shadow of a commitment without the real thing. Neither wanted another relationship, but they were incapable of being emotionally transparent because of their rampant conflict and Tom's lack of emotional commitment in their marriage. They were physically committed to one another for better or worse, but they weren't close to enjoying the full benefits of relational unity.

Physical commitment without emotional intimacy was not worth much to Tom and Jan. Intimacy without commitment had limited value for Todd and Cindy. Both ingredients are needed to build a strong relationship, and they are integrally connected. Sadly, most marriages lack one or the other. Without both commitment and emotional vulnerability, our relationships and marriages will lack zest and vitality. We will always feel disappointed and discouraged, painfully aware that something is missing.

This book will help you find a man who will be committed to you. It will help you learn to make healthy choices in a man, to recognize when someone is willing to be emotionally committed to you. If you are already in a relationship, you'll see why your man may be frightened of doing that. You will also look at your own commitment issues and then take the risk of all risks by willingly writing your partner or spouse into your future life story. These issues are crucial for everyone.

Let's face it: Issues of commitment are at the root of many relational problems. Have you ever found yourself...

- desiring closeness but finding your man unwilling to give it?
- being with a man who offered myriad excuses for not spending quality time with you?

- enjoying a loving evening but then feeling distanced and rejected the next day?
- desiring a commitment but being with someone unwilling to give it?
- wanting to be attached but being with a man who was resistant to making long-range plans that involve both of you?
- being discouraged and settling for a relationship without long-term commitment?
- filling up your life until you have no room left for closeness and commitment?

Immortal Love

Cindy is disillusioned, worried about her future. Jan and Tom struggle with ongoing feelings of discouragement. Their memories of early days of relational bliss grow faint. Can you remember yours?

Do you remember the day you met your man, the way your eyes danced with delight? You felt the wonderful quivering of attraction. Horizons seemed boundless. Sunsets were never more vibrant. Sunrises held forever promises.

Time brought up times and down times, but the relationship moved forward. You expected tough times. You remembered earlier counsel not to expect to feel romantic and "in love" every minute of every day. You could deal with the waxing and waning of emotional rush. But you weren't prepared for this—a man who could not commit. A relationship with all the ingredients to make lifelong love a possibility but without the critical ingredient of commitment. How could immortal love blossom in this arid climate?

Few brides walk down the aisle believing that if the marriage doesn't work out, they still have other options. Few men anticipate anything in their marriage or relationship that will cause them enough pain to make them pull back like a turtle hiding in its shell. Neither expects that the issues of commitment or emotional vulnerability will cause problems.

But far too often, the enchanted forest becomes less than enchanting. You gradually begin to withdraw your love in response to disappointment in your marriage. Without emotional and physical commitment, you may not pull out completely—just enough to create an emotional barrier of protection. He may not leave either—instead, he may become overly involved in work or fail to put sufficient effort into dealing with intimacy and emotional vulnerability. And so the relationship stagnates.

Commitment Is Difficult

As a youth, I could not make the commitment, small as it was, to risk my parents' wrath to enjoy an adventure with my friends. Though the cost would have been relatively minor, I flinched instead of taking the plunge. Later, as a teen, I flinched again instead of expressing my budding, naïvely youthful affection for Karen.

An adult commitment to a mate is a much larger issue. No wonder so many men balk and end up losing out on the inherent joys of a fully developed relationship. Many men seem able to make the initial step but then falter along the way.

Perhaps you have agreed to commit yourself to marriage, only to find yourself reconsidering because the relationship lacks intimacy. Perhaps your man says he is committed but secretly retains the option of leaving if the going gets rough. And you sense it! If so, you are not alone. This is common today.

Bookstores offer us a panoply of options to help us understand why men won't commit, why partners cheat, and why communication can be so difficult. We all know of marriages that have failed, men who refused to grow up, and spouses who languished in a relationship that died years ago. We realize that building a meaningful relationship can be difficult, but it is impossible without physical and emotional commitment. These ingredients are not optional, decorative icing on a cake—they are the cake.

If you want to learn more about your man and his aversion to commitment, this book will give you hope. It will help transform an agonizingly push-pull dance into a harmonious waltz—if he proves willing. You will soon be ready to make an accurate and healthy assessment of his ability to commit, and if he is unwilling and you are not yet married, how to say goodbye and move on.

Real Commitment

As you consider the issue of commitment and your man's many distancing maneuvers, take some time to look at your own behaviors as well. Eileen Silva Kindig, in her book *Goodbye Prince Charming*, examines the issues involved in commitment, especially in marriage. She suggests that we fail to truly understand what is involved when we say, "I do." She challenges both partners to reconsider the importance of commitment and emotional vulnerability. Who cannot relate to her words?

> Certainly it would be easier sometimes not to be burdened by the demands of marriage...But unless we care deeply for someone other than ourselves, our lives become shallow and empty. There comes a point when gratifying our every whim becomes more of a prison than a panacea. Yet this is one thing the Cinderella myth fails to address. Romantic fantasy concerns itself so exclusively with what Prince Charming is supposed to be giving us that it fails to address what we're supposed to be giving in return.[4]

Ouch! Kindig's words sting. *I thought it was all about me!* I thought I was supposed to focus on what I need, what I want, and how to get the world to respond accordingly. Could Kindig be right about the shallowness of selfish living? Might we find real meaning in our relationship only when we tackle the rugged roadblocks to commitment and emotional vulnerability? Does a bit of reserve hide beneath the surface of your apparent willingness to commit?

Kindig says that without commitment "there is little to keep us believing in marriage once the lights go out and the music stops playing." Who has not been in a marriage or relationship only to be dumbfounded when the romantic music stopped and our hearts quit palpitating when our beloved drove into the driveway? Who has not been surprised by the anger on display the first time we fought? Where did these feelings come from?

Kindig shares the underlying causes.

> Commitment must not be confused with obligation, however. Many people say they're committed to marriage, yet live in abject misery. That's because they're really committed to something different: their children, their religious beliefs, their self-image, their reputation, their lifestyle, or even the idea of marriage. To find the satisfaction we seek in a lifelong relationship we have to be committed to the person we chose to be our partner.

The Freedom of Commitment

I approach this book unashamedly espousing the benefits of commitment—not just because I believe it to be the deepest desire of God and a reflection of His commitment to us, but because it has so many benefits.

Perhaps instead of being afraid of commitment and emotional vulnerability, we can envision the freedom that comes from this higher calling. Instead of making us feel trapped and shackled, maybe our relationship can free us. This might be a tough sell for many men, but I offer the following insights for those willing to reconsider the risk-to-benefit ratio of commitment and emotional vulnerability.

In his book *Love and Survival*, Dean Ornish talks about the freedom that comes with commitment:

> Commitment leads to real freedom, in any arena. This is particularly true in relationships of all kinds, for you can only be intimate to the degree that you can be vulnerable. You can only be vulnerable and open your heart to the degree that you feel safe—because if you make yourself vulnerable, you might get hurt. Commitment creates safety and makes intimacy possible.[5]

Ornish challenges us with these questions:

- Do you want to be vulnerable to another?
- Do you want to create safety in your relationship?
- Do you really want to be known and know your mate?
- Do you want a safe place to share your hurts, pains, joys, and sorrows?

You absolutely must answer these questions candidly. Take some time to decide if this is really what you want. Then have a candid conversation with your man.

Why do I challenge you to wrestle with these questions before moving forward? Because my experience has shown that many men and women will quickly announce that they want intimacy, only to act in ways that sabotage it. Many people say they want to be close to their mates but have never known safety and intimacy and have no idea how to achieve it.

I offer Ornish's comments here, not as the ideal that we should try to emulate but as the first step toward learning the language of intimacy, emotional vulnerability, and commitment. As you take this glimpse into his marriage, make a few notes. Ask yourself the following questions and be prepared for a few surprises in your answers.

- Do I want this level of honesty in my marriage?
- Do I want this kind of intimacy?
- Do I want to be committed to my mate?
- Will I demand the following level of commitment from my mate?

I commit myself fully to you, for I want this relationship to be as intimate and loving as possible. Our intimacy and love nourish my soul and allow me to experience the most happiness and meaning.

I am willing to risk making myself more and more vulnerable to you, even though I may get hurt from time to time. I would rather take that risk and have the potential of real intimacy than to wall myself off and have the certainty of being isolated and alone.

I commit to being completely and totally honest with you, for we can be open and vulnerable with each other only if we can fully trust each other.

I commit to try to avoid hurting you so that we can create something really sacred. I know there will be times where we may hurt each other, knowingly or unknowingly, but I will do my best to not cause you pain. When that happens, I will ask for your forgiveness and I will offer mine without reservation. When we can make mistakes in a relationship that has become safe and sacred, then knowing we can love and be loved even when we mess up builds even greater trust, makes it feel even safer, and deepens the intimacy.[6]

There it is—the revelation of a man laying it on the line. Ornish is able to say, "I'm in. I'm willing to be emotionally present to you and to write you into my future."

For me, this is exhilarating, heady, and scary stuff. I am tempted to wonder, *This guy is the leading authority on mind-body health and has a national audience. But does it really work like this for him behind the scenes, when the lights are down and the audience has gone home?*

As I read about Ornish's commitment to his bride, I am filled with excitement, envy, and wonder. Could this level of closeness and attachment possibly be available to all? I am convinced that it is.

I Am My Beloved's

As profound as Ornish's advice is, it is hardly new. He has said nothing that the Scriptures have not already said. You will recall that God instituted companionship, intimacy, and marriage, and He declared that the two will become one flesh (Genesis 2:24) This, of course, has profound implications for every couple. No longer will they retain two completely independent identities. Instead, they will become one. The emotional closeness and complete commitment pictured in the Garden can be yours. God wants you to enjoy them.

The Scriptures offer many other examples of the committed relationship. Consider the commitment Jonathan made to David. "Jonathan made a covenant with David because he loved him as himself. Jonathan took off the robe he was wearing and gave it to David, along with his tunic, and even his sword, his bow and his belt"(1 Samuel 18:3-4). The story of Jonathan and David is replete with examples of self-sacrifice. They enjoyed a deep and abiding friendship because of their commitment to one another.

Consider the commitment Ruth made to Naomi. Both women were widowed and thus incredibly vulnerable. Ruth, who was younger and could still find a husband to provide protection, made a decision to stand by her mother-in-law. Her act of loyalty is legendary.

"Don't urge me to leave you or turn back from you. Where you go I will go, and where you stay I will stay. Your people will be my people and your God, my God. Where you die I will die, and there I will be buried" (Ruth 1:16-17). Though these words are from a daughter-in-law to a mother-in-law, they are common in marriage ceremonies because they so effectively describe the commitment required in healthy marriages.

Finally, consider the commitment we see in the Song of Solomon. "My lover is mine, and I am his." Simple. Profound. Delightful. Here we see a sense of ownership and belonging. One person belongs exclusively to another for all time. That is worth aspiring to. It's available to you.

Are you working toward a committed relationship? Will you consider writing your mate into your personal future and expect no less from him? Will you learn all you can about barriers to commitment, the steps to healthy commitment, and your own issues in this area? Are you and your partner ready to develop a new level of emotional intimacy?

Let's journey together toward our personal goal—one person belonging completely and exclusively to another.

ONE

LIVING WHAT HE'S LEARNED

*Love, in the fullest and most concrete sense of the word…
seems to rest on the unconditional: I shall continue to love
you no matter what happens…Love, far from requiring
the acceptance of risk, demands it. Love seems to be calling
for a challenge to be tested because it is sure to emerge the
conqueror.*

GABRIEL MARCEL

We often live what we learn. Men who won't commit often come from backgrounds that may explain their difficulties with commitment phobia. Those who were raised in broken homes often seem to expect that this will also happen to them. Men who have been hurt badly in childhood by their parents' divorce, and have not resolved their issues with it, carry their struggles into their adult relationships.

Jim sat quietly across from me, staring blankly out the office window. A tall, burly man, he was fit and sturdy from throwing 100-pound bags of grain around at the local feed store. He wore stained Carhartt overalls and a baseball cap with a curled brim that covered a full head of jet-black hair.

Jim did not want to be in my office. He was angry about his circumstances—his second wife had told him to get help, or their marriage was in jeopardy. He felt blackmailed, cornered, and judged. What was so wrong with him that he should be ordered to see a psychologist? How had things gotten so far out of control?

Jim and his wife, Tina, had come to see me several months earlier when she had run out of patience with him. Tired of his profanity, angry outbursts, and volatile temper with her young daughter and his sons, she insisted they get some counseling to try to save their five-year marriage.

"I am so tired of telling him how to behave," she had said sadly. "I already have a child to raise—I sure don't want to raise him. I want to be with a man I can respect, and it's hard to respect a man who can't manage his own moods."

Tina shared that she was reluctantly exploring the possibility of a separation, which annoyed Jim even more. She shared her irritation that he seemed insensitive to the possible separation and problems leading to it—even taunting her several times to go ahead with it. He showed little commitment to work on the serious issues in their relationship. Tina questioned how much Jim really cared for her and her daughter, and in fact, how close he was to his sons.

Months earlier I had sat with them, exploring their brief, vibrant courtship and the unification of his family with hers. They shared how their marriage had started out wonderfully. Both 30 years old and recovering from failed marriages, they were immediately attracted to each other. They were ready for another chance at love, marriage, and family.

Jim brought two young sons into the relationship. They lived with his ex-wife but visited Jim every other weekend. Tina had a three-year-old daughter in her permanent custody. The children enjoyed being together and felt invigorated to be part of a whole family. Both Jim and Tina felt like they had finished grieving their lost marriages and were now ready to give commitment another try.

Jim and Tina had spent time in counseling during their previous marriages, with very different results. Tina felt that she had learned some things during counseling. Although the marriage ultimately failed, she felt stronger and wiser for the effort. Jim, on the other hand, believed that attending marriage counseling with his ex had been a waste of time. Although he discovered some of the mistakes he was making, he hadn't liked the previous counselor and was tentative about coming to see me.

Jim and Tina agreed on one thing—they did not want to repeat the mistakes of their first marriages. Yet here they were, discouraged, disillusioned, and wondering once again if they needed to begin emotionally preparing for divorce court.

After spending a few sessions with Jim and Tina, I was now working primarily with Jim. He clearly needed to see me alone because most of Tina's complaints appeared accurate.

Jim seemed demanding, uptight, and tense much of the time. He appeared to have rigid expectations of their children, and this simply would not work in their blended family. He ran the family the way he ran the feed store—methodically, practically, failing to take Tina's parenting requests into consideration. Tina was wounded, and her heart was hardening. She was ready to separate even though that prospect was painful to her. She still loved Jim, but her first loyalty was to her daughter, who had begun to show symptoms of depression as a result of Jim's nonstop criticism. Tina was reluctantly willing to sacrifice their marriage if that was what it took to help her daughter.

Jim sat expressionless before me. I was surprised at his apparent detached manner.

"So, Jim, how have you and Tina been doing?"

"Tina is thinking about a separation," he said gruffly. "I don't like it, but I guess that's how it's going to be."

"Do you have any idea why she has decided on a separation?" I wondered if he could now see that his critical, detached attitude was pushing her away from him.

"Tina wants things to be perfect," he blurted angrily. "She wants me to come home from the store, smile when I walk in the door, and tell everyone what a wonderful day I've had. That's a lot to ask. I work hard, and I'm tired when I get home."

"Tell me about your moods," I said.

"Sure, I'm moody. Who wouldn't be? My wife is threatening me with a separation, and I won't put my boys through that again. They've been through one divorce, and I swore they'd never experience that again. If she wants a separation, that's it. Let her separate from me. I don't want it, but I can live with it."

I watched Jim stiffen as he talked about his marriage and his twisted perceptions of Tina's expectations. I wondered how much fear and sadness might be behind his surface anger.

"Are you sad at all about what is happening to you and Tina?" I asked. "You told me you were hoping this would be a second chance for both of you. How do you feel now?"

"Yeah, I guess I'm sad. I'm real sad. But I've been through it before. I know what to expect. I know how to set up my own home, and I can get along just fine without her. If that's what she wants, that's what she'll get. I hope she knows what she's doing. As for me, I'll cope with it. I'll be fine."

Again, Jim's anger was apparent. He was tight-lipped, surly, and sarcastic. I wondered how much hurt lay beneath the surface and what its real source might be.

"Jim," I said, "you are acting tough and detached, as though the threat of Tina and her daughter leaving means nothing to you.

I can't believe that is true. You've already lost one marriage and can't be too happy about the prospect of losing another. What's going on?"

"Sure, I care." He leaned forward, propping his arms on his knees. "But she's going to do what she's going to do, regardless of what I say or think. I'm working as hard on this marriage as I can, and it doesn't seem to make much difference. I went through this as a kid. It seems like it's just part of life."

"Jim," I asked, "are you willing to make any adjustments for Tina? You seem like you've already taken this marriage into divorce court."

"Well, I'm willing to work at it. I wonder, though, if it will do any good. Sometimes it seems hopeless. Nothing worked out for my parents. Why should it work out for me?"

"Let's talk about the early years of your life, Jim. Sounds like that might have something to do with your reaction to Tina right now."

Jim's mood shifted abruptly when I brought up his past. He started to fidget and his eyes became moist with tears he could barely contain. I had struck a nerve.

"I still hate my parents for what they did to us kids. My life ended when I was ten."

Jim wiped a tear from his eyes, looked over at me, and continued.

"My mom and dad divorced when I was ten. I lived with my mom and could only see my dad every other weekend. He meant a lot to me, but instead of being with him, I watched Mom parade one man after another through the house.

"She married two more times before I graduated from high school. I wasn't close to any of the men—and they didn't seem to really care about me. I learned pretty quick to keep my bags packed because nobody was going to take care of me but me. Seems like things haven't change a whole lot."

"It sounds like you really suffered," I said. "Kids need and deserve stability in their lives. You were a good kid and those were vulnerable years."

"They could have been fabulous years for me," he continued. "I could have excelled in school, and I was just starting to do well in sports. But Mom and Dad screwed that up for me. I always had to wonder who would be coming into my mom's life next."

"So what about your dad?"

"He wasn't a lot better than Mom. He never married again, but he dated so many women I couldn't keep them straight. He tried to show an interest in my sports and things, but he was working a lot, and when he wasn't working he was out with his friends or girlfriends. I got shortchanged, that's for sure. So, Doc, you can see why this latest episode with Tina doesn't faze me. I handled it before and I can handle it now."

As I watched Jim, I pictured a 30-year-old man packing around a damaged boy inside. Thirty years old going on ten. The fragile heart that had been wounded long ago was facing another loss. Jim was preparing himself for the worst.

What Jim didn't know or couldn't see was that the defenses he was using to prevent further pain were propelling him toward the very thing that frightened him. Surely, without significant intervention, he would find himself back in divorce court. Once again, he would be alone with nothing to guide him but an entrenched view of a hostile, uncommitted, detached world.

Nevada Street

As I listened to Jim, I remembered my own life at ten years old. When Jim was ten, he faced a harsh world that would affect him profoundly. People entered and departed his life at will. My world, thankfully, was quite different. However, it still contained enough reality to destroy my naïveté about the world.

I grew up in a small town near the Canadian border in Washington state. The community was heavily influenced by the logging industry. Even at an early age, I was interested in how families functioned. I wondered how my family compared with others. I suppose many children wonder about these things. *Is their family as happy as mine? Do they have more money? Does their dad work as hard as mine?*

Walking up and down Nevada Street, I took in everything I could about the families. I noticed that my next-door neighbors, the Silsbees, seemed very happy. The three boys, all friends of mine, had a mother and father who seemed to care about them. They had curfews, ate dinner together, and attended church every Sunday. I felt safe and comfortable with them because their home provided a caring and loving environment.

Up the street were the Johnsons, the Stephenses, and the Rosenthals. Their families also seemed very much like mine. Each had two parents, often a mom who was a homemaker or who worked part-time and a dad who worked outside the home. Each family had a couple of kids. Most attended church on Sunday. These were families like mine with kids like me. We shared a way of life in our small, close-knit community.

But down a few doors were the Kilgers, and life in their home was quite different. Tommy's parents had divorced years ago, and he was now living with his dad, stepmother, and stepbrother.

Tommy never really liked his stepbrother, Jimmy, and they fought a lot. Tommy was our age, but Jimmy was younger, and we never wanted him to play with us. Tommy told me that he didn't like not having a choice about Jimmy joining their family. Jimmy was a bratty, demanding kid who did not know how to blend in. In spite of being younger, he wanted to boss us around, and that was not going to happen. In time we came to accept him but never as one of our close friends.

I remember feeling awkward in the Kilgers' home. Tommy's stepmother always seemed distant. Now I know she was struggling with her husband's problem with alcohol as well as the issues that inevitably come with stepparenting. She didn't have an easy job. Even with the tension that I knew existed in their marriage, the Kilgers were trying to make their family work.

The Kilgers offered me one of my first lessons about family life gone awry. I witnessed firsthand the impact of divorce and the difficulty of blending second families. I could see that not every child lived with their parents on a quiet street, free from problems that create distance and detachment. Tommy did not have the security that comes from growing up in a stable family. He seemed insecure, restless, and overly competitive, which I suspect was a result of instability in his home.

Once I realized what was happening with the Kilgers, I was even happier with my family. In spite of three sisters and an older brother who were definitely challenges to me (and I to them!), we were a cohesive, loving family. Perfect? No. But we were an army against the world when the chips were down. My brother came to my rescue in neighborhood squabbles, and I always had an underlying pride in being associated with my siblings. We had family commitment.

We were also committed to our church family, which was an integral part of our lives rather than an appendage. I would not fully understand the powerful influence this would have on my life until much later.

I didn't know what living in a blended family felt like. I didn't know the pain of divorce. I didn't know how much damage alcoholism could do. I felt protected and safe with parents who I knew loved each other and were committed to one another for life. Simply by observing their behavior, I came to know affection and intimacy firsthand. This helped set the stage for what I would expect as an adult.

Fragmented Society

My childhood experience on Nevada Street is not representative of what is happening in much of America today. I grew up during a time that featured safe towns and a low divorce rate.

We knew our neighbors. Marriages and families were stable, filled with security and commitment. Lest you think I was raised without running water or electricity or that we walked without shoes to and from school, that was not the case. Life was, however, quite idyllic.

Things have certainly changed some since my days on Nevada Street. With today's high divorce rate, many children are denied the stability and predictability of a traditional nuclear family. Studies have shown that only 12 in 100 children in 1950 came from broken families, whereas 58 out of 100 lived in broken homes in 1992. That number still appears to be climbing.

Although we may try to assuage our guilt about our contribution to these statistics and minimize their relevance, they should make us pause. We know that children who grow up in broken homes are more likely to have other problems, including academic issues, criminal involvement, and—as highlighted in this book—fear of commitment. An atmosphere of alienation and distance exists in today's society. It has weakened people's obligation to one another and to their families.

Noted researcher and author Judith Wallerstein, in her book *The Unexpected Legacy of Divorce,* challenges us to reexamine divorce. She points out that we have been taught to believe that divorce may be difficult for children but not devastating. A broken family, we once believed, need not have a detrimental effect on children.

Wallerstein challenges this perspective. She found that children of divorce struggled to develop healthy, committed relationships as adults. Wallerstein noted that divorce may free the parents, but it traps children in a quagmire of consequences that often linger for years. Some of the most dramatic consequences have to do with lack of commitment in relationships and difficulties with emotional intimacy.

Attachment and Fear

Fragmented society.

Broken homes.

Divorce.

Men who will not commit.

Sadly, these puzzle pieces often fit together. On the other hand, a stable home life helps people develop healthy attitudes about attachment, intimacy, and commitment.

Researchers have known for a long time that a secure environment during our early years provides us with the safety we need to create positive attachments to our caregivers. In that secure attachment we are able to create a healthy identity, and this is the basis for our adult relationships. When early life is unstable and chaotic, adult relationships are likely to be the same.

Dr. Laura Schlessinger, in her book *Ten Stupid Things Women Do to Mess Up Their Lives,* states, "Your personal insecurity is a reaction to the very real and repetitive abandonment and consequent insecurity that marked your childhood."[1]

Jim is an apt example of what happens to people who are wounded at a young age. His parents' divorce was a critical turning point in his life. It was not the divorce alone that damaged him. It was also the conflict and instability prior to the divorce. The decline in his relationship with his father after the divorce contributed as much to the problem as his changed relationship with his mother.

Jim's mother was forced to work harder to provide financial stability for the family. She grieved the loss of her marriage and then began dating, taking her away from children who desperately needed her attention. She married men who would become Jim's stepfathers. To this day, he struggles with his loss of self-esteem. He was wounded badly as a child and has been carrying around those wounds for years. He now experiences serious problems with attachment, commitment, and intimacy as a result. He is detached and uncommitted to himself and others.

The Agony of Commitment and Vows

The conflict and fragmentation in our society, not to mention the dangers that can befall a relationship, can make us think twice before making a lasting commitment. We look around and see marriages failing at a precipitous rate. Friends we thought would stay together forever are simply giving up on their relationships. Young people are rethinking their options—including whether they want to make a commitment to one person after what they have seen in their parents' generation. Sadly, even long-term marriages are failing at horrific rates. More and more women seem to be questioning whether marriage is truly meeting their needs.

Considering the larger societal issues, we can see why men (and women) might struggle with commitment. Sam Keen, in his book *To Love and Be Loved,* provides valuable counsel:

> The specter of binding ourselves to cherish and care for a friend, a child, a lover, a mate, in an unknown future arouses our fears of being imprisoned within a space too small for our spirit. Every commitment is based on a decision, a choice of one alternative to the exclusion of others. Making a commitment involves self-sacrifice, voluntary self-limitation, and cutting off future possibilities. So it doesn't seem prudent to pledge fidelity without qualifications. How can I promise to maintain a relationship without risking a betrayal of myself? What if my feelings change? The risk of commitment arouses anxiety, which can be faced only with courage and the resolve to further the long-range fortunes of love.[2]

Keen is highlighting what many men seem to feel when dealing with the prospect of making a commitment to someone, but he is certainly not promoting the uncommitted life. Hardly. Listen to what he says:

Certainly it is risky to promise that we will continue to care for our children, our friends, our mates, to bind ourselves to conditions we cannot predict. But consider what will become of us if we do not! To cobble together a life without commitments, a life of one-night stands, tentative relationships, and limited engagements is a guarantee of superficiality and loneliness. Entangling alliances may bind us too closely for comfort, but life without entwinement is as fragile as a rope of sand. Without abiding commitments and vows, there are arrangements but no marriages, child care but no families, associations but no friendships, housing developments but no communities, a present but no memory of the past or hope for the future, a collection of experiences but no spirit or soul.[3]

Superficiality of Vows

We can understand why men who have already experienced brokenness in a marriage are wary about making the Grand Commitment. Certainly you have felt some of those feelings yourself. Commitment is scary business. But men seem willing to make a vow in their hearts—for as long as the relationship will sustain itself. They are committed until they are not committed—and this is infuriating.

Perhaps your man has a superficial approach to commitment. Perhaps you have even abandoned the "forever" idea yourself, partially in response to his timidity. I understand. In fact, most of us understand because at some level we have all wrestled with the issue of commitment. Many people bear the scars of divorce, unsafe neighborhoods, broken friendships, and an absence of parental love. Who has not felt the touch of the fragmentary nature of our society?

Perhaps you, like my client Jim, have been wounded by early family experiences that have tainted your perception of everything related to commitment and vows. Whether or not you feel safe in making the plunge, you no doubt see that superficial vows lack substance. They lack spirit and soul. Without commitment, you are in a relationship held together with frayed twine.

To hold back on the issue of commitment, to keep a governor on the accelerator of relating, slows us down. We cannot be fully engaged when we have one foot on the brake. It is like agreeing to a pact with a handshake while our fingers are crossed behind our back.

But why is making a vow to another so critical? Why is this something you long for and should be willing to work for in your relationship? Let's listen once again to Keen:

> The taking of vows lifts commitment from the private to the public, from the tentative to the absolute, from the secular to the sacred. Traditionally, marriage vows are not between two individuals but are promises made in the presence of family and community. The witnesses to vows form a third party in the relationship. That we pledge fidelity in a formal and public ceremony is a recognition that a marriage between a couple can thrive only within a context of family, friends, and community.[4]

Making a commitment to another person changes the relationship. We may tell ourselves that it's really nothing more than "a piece of paper," but this simply is not true. Many things change, which is part of the reason many men resist taking that step. When we make the decision to commit ourselves to another, we no longer remain hidden behind our facade of propriety. We let our shadow sides come out, for better or for worse. We become invested in this marriage and are willing to let ourselves be real.

Our differences, seemingly obvious before, now are even more apparent. But in the realness of committed marriage, we stand a chance of being completely loved and accepted. In spite of our differences, in committed marriage we will allow ourselves to be different, and that will be okay. You say potato and I say potahto.

An Insidious Attitude

Take a normal, healthy relationship, add the cost and risk of a growing commitment, and we can understand why a man might back away. Rather than commit, he works to keep his options open, or moves to keep from being hemmed in. *If she is going to wax when I wane, why bother?* he wonders. *If he is going to zig when I zag, I want some space,* she considers. *Perhaps detachment really isn't so bad,* Jim tells himself. If ultimate hurt and loss is the outcome, he wonders if a committed relationship is worth the effort.

In most cases, the attitude of detachment, often stemming in large part from family upbringing, is an insidious thing. Consider another client's plight.

Susan was a 30-year-old accountant who had yet to marry. She came in for counseling because she wanted to find out "if anything is wrong with me for not being married yet." People who are dating frequently voice frustrations like hers—more people are waiting longer to marry, but they're not necessarily happy about doing so. A nagging sense of doubt impedes their progress.

Susan was a bright woman and dressed well. She was articulate, stating clearly that she wanted to be married and have children but that she was anxious about her biological clock ticking. She explained that she previously had several serious relationships, but none came close to leading to marriage. She now wondered if she had wasted her time in these steady relationships when she could have been looking for a more suitable marriage partner.

As we explored Susan's history, I discovered it was similar to Jim's—her parents had divorced when she was four years old, and she had been raised by her mother. Susan explained that she was much closer to her mother than her father because he lived across the country, and she only visited him for a few weeks during the summers.

In counseling we explored Susan's expectations of marriage. She told me she always intended to establish her career before even thinking about having children. She certainly had done that. She also expressed worries about her ability to commit, having seen her father work his way through a series of girlfriends before remarrying.

Susan felt a sense of uneasiness. Previously, she had been adamant about remaining childless, but recently the urge for children hit her rather suddenly. Now, at 30, she was dreaming of marriage without having a suitor, desiring children without having a prospective father. She felt detached and discouraged.

Susan has learned a lot in counseling, much of which she did not realize was affecting her decisions regarding a mate. She recognizes now that she may have picked up some unhealthy attitudes from her parents and from society at large. She learned, vicariously and insidiously, that marriage is not necessarily permanent and that many people do not take it all that seriously. She learned that relationships come and go and that she should be cautious about becoming involved. She has come to see that these attitudes do not fit with her Christian faith and wants to change them. She has come to see that God, the Father, is committed to her, and committed, covenantal marriage is part of His plan. She wants to find a man with whom she can share her values, her life, and her children. She is becoming ready for attachment, closeness, and commitment.

Healing Our Society

Although we cannot change society as a whole, we can do our part to heal our little corner of it—including ourselves and our relationships. Let's talk about what each of us can do to positively influence our world and also examine how this will help with the issues of commitment and intimacy.

Work on healing yourself. You are an integral part of a community, and a community is only as healthy as its individual parts. You come into contact with many people every day. As you commit yourself to your own healing, specifically the subtle attitudes and destructive patterns that inhibit you from attaching to others or choosing a healthy mate, you do your part to change the world.

Work on healing your relationships. You can work on creating healthy relationships. You can choose to surround yourself with healthy people and to be healthy with those people. You can dedicate yourself to being in relationship only with men of integrity—those who exhibit honesty, moral fiber, healthy boundaries, and the ability to commit to one woman.

If you are married, you have an opportunity to fully commit yourself to your marriage and to expect that from your man. Consider how you may be holding back from really attaching yourself to your mate or how you may be enabling him to avoid fully committing himself. Consider the secrets you may still be keeping or his problems you may be trying to ignore, and examine the ways you can become more honest. Reflect on strategies that will assist both of you to become more intimate and transparent in your marriage. As you do this, you will influence your man and the world around you.

Work on healing your family. Because you are an adult, you may believe you can't do anything to affect your family of origin, but that is not true. Your family is still dynamic, ever-changing. If you adjust the way you relate to your parents and siblings, they will change too. Consider the old ways you related to them and how you might now communicate more effectively. As you change the way you connect with your family, you also change your part of the world for the better. When you set healthy boundaries with your family and communicate more effectively, you also improve your relationship with your man.

Work on healing your church. Yes, your church probably exhibits some qualities of a dysfunctional family. Because it is made up of people like you and me, it will naturally mirror the problems of our larger society. Your church is therefore an excellent place to practice self-disclosure, honesty, transparency, and commitment. When we practice those things, we heal ourselves, our relationships, our marriages, and our families. We will also be transforming our churches, making them important change agents for society.

Work on healing your community. You have an opportunity to get more involved and committed to your community. It will take on the shape and character of those who choose to get involved. Perhaps you can find a way to use your talents and gifts to positively impact your community. Consider where you might become more attached, where you might volunteer to make a positive change in your community.

Jesus, Society, and Commitment

The issue of commitment winds through the Scripture, always in the context of relationships or the community as a whole. This book is about commitment and intimacy in relationships, but the crisis fans out far beyond this narrow but important scope. We are a society that fears commitment to nearly anything, including our mates. Consider these truths:

- We tend to jump from friendship to friendship.
- We tend to jump from church to church.
- We tend to jump from job to job.
- We tend to jump from group to group.
- We tend to jump from spouse to spouse.

And the whole time we can never develop any depth or richness in relationships. We never really place both feet inside the circle of our personal relationships.

The Bible teaches us that commitments are important. When we make a commitment to our mate, Jesus implores us to keep it. He wants us to be committed to whatever good we under-take—and He wants us to be committed to one another. Consider the earliest Christians' example:

> They devoted themselves to the apostles' teaching and to the fellowship, to the breaking of bread and to prayer. Everyone was filled with awe, and many wonders and miraculous signs were done by the apostles. All the believers were together and had everything in common. Selling their possessions and goods, they gave to anyone as he had need. Every day they continued to meet together in the temple courts. They broke bread in their homes and ate together with glad and sincere hearts, praising God and enjoying the favor of all the people. And the Lord added to their number daily those who were being saved (Acts 2:42-47).

This story is almost incomprehensible today, especially to men. Selling our prized possessions and giving to others in need? This goes against every capitalistic bone in our bodies. Men particularly feel that they work hard for what is theirs and are reluctant to share it. Yet men need to learn more about sharing their time and money. They must learn that as they care for others, they also care for themselves. As much as men like Jim want to believe that they can make it alone just fine, this simply is not true.

You may have heard the story about a party that took place aboard a cruise ship. Sitting at the table of honor was a 70-year-old man. Earlier that morning a young woman had fallen overboard, and within seconds this elderly gentleman was in the cold, dark waters at her side. He rescued the woman and became an instant hero.

After the sumptuous meal, the captain and crew made speeches. When the time came for the brave gentleman to speak, the room fell quiet in anticipation. He rose from his chair, went to the microphone, and said, "I just want to know one thing: Who pushed me?"

Many of us can relate to this story. We often finally commit to something only after being cajoled, persuaded, pushed, or threatened to take action. We are reluctant heroes. This is especially true with commitment and intimacy in our relationships and marriage. We are often hesitant participants.

Jim needed to be pushed to strengthen his commitment to Tina. In counseling, we discovered that he had gone into his marriage with less than a heartfelt commitment and was ready to run as soon as the going got tough. He hadn't recognized his superficial commitment until he felt uncomfortable and was threatened with another divorce. Rather than struggle with some difficult personality traits as well as thorny blended-family problems, his first option was to seek refuge in what had been comfortable for him: detachment. But that was not what he really wanted, and he worked for months to heal his old family issues so he could be fully present to Tina. Today, he continues to make progress in counseling and has renewed his commitment to Tina, their marriage, and their blended family. He decided that his marriage is worth saving, and he's working hard to do just that.

God is neither a hesitant participant nor a reluctant hero in our lives. As the author of relationships, He initiated a committed relationship to each of us. While we were still sinners, Christ chose to die for us. And He didn't stop there. He made us children of God:

> For you did not receive a spirit that makes you a slave again to fear, but you received the Spirit of sonship. And by him we cry "Abba, Father." The Spirit himself testifies with our spirit that we are God's children. Now if we are children, then we are heirs—heirs of God and co-heirs with Christ, if indeed we share in his sufferings in order that we may also share in his glory (Romans 8:15-17).

He jumped into some pretty cold waters to save us—and is committed to us regardless of the challenges we might present.

Final Thoughts

The malady is detachment, so the remedy is attachment. Easier said than done—or is it? Perhaps all we need to do, what men need to do, is reconnect to one another and commit ourselves to doing so forever.

I was amused recently when watching the movie *Shall We Dance?* Susan Sarandon plays the sophisticated but too predictable wife of debonair but bored Richard Gere. He reaches a point of quiet desperation and secretly takes up dance lessons, which certainly spices up his life. She fears the worst and has a private detective trace his movements, only to discover that he is involved with dancing, not the dreaded affair.

In a poignant segment of the movie, she discusses why he might have taken these actions. She is asked why she married him in the first place and what might be missing for him and her now.

> Because we need a witness to our lives. There are over a million people on the planet and we need someone to witness our lives. In a marriage you're promising to care about everything; the good things, the bad things, the terrible things, the mundane things. All of it. All the time, every day. You're saying your life will not go unnoticed, because I will notice it. Your life will not go unwitnessed, because I will witness it.

Maybe it's just that simple. Maybe a large part of our role in relationships and marriage is making sure we notice what happens with us and our mate. As you encourage your man to lovingly notice and tend to your life, in small steps, by paying close and special attention, you both will begin to heal the sense of detachment that pervades your home, family, and community.

Loving attention heals. Try it. We will explore how to receive that from your man as well.

TWO

FALLING SHORT
OF GREAT EXPECTATIONS

―――――

Forgetting what is behind and straining toward what is ahead, I press on toward the goal to win the prize for which God has called me heavenward in Christ Jesus.

PHILIPPIANS 3:13-14

Disappointment is part of life. What we do about it is optional.

Our world measures the margin of victory in thousandths of a second, leaving no room for doubt, discouragement, or disbelief. That's why Olympians must learn to direct their minds to coax every possible bit of energy, learning, and perseverance out of their bodies. True competitors must believe they are champions, entitled to perform on this prestigious world stage.

Dan Jansen was this kind of champion. You may recall that this hero did not succeed at first, but he eventually proved he had the drive and unaltered commitment to achieve the gold. His path to victory was neither easy nor direct.

In the 1988 Olympics, Jansen was the world speed skating champion and the heavy favorite to take home the gold in both the 500- and 1000-meter events. He had trained for years, putting in countless hours of preparation. But on the very day he was to compete in the 500, his sister, Jane Beres, died of leukemia. This overwhelmingly emotional situation was too much for his psyche. He entered the competition with a lion on his back—and he buckled under the pressure.

Less than ten seconds into the race, he fell rounding a turn, slid off the track, and was eliminated from the race. Jansen and his adoring fans were crushed. The cameras revealed a man struggling to keep his composure. Three days later he was unable to shake the disaster from his mind, falling again in the 1000-meter race and failing to finish. Dispirited and dejected, he went home without a medal but not without hope.

Most would have given up at this point. Most would have settled for the accolades he had achieved in earlier competitions. But not Jansen. He had a singular commitment—he wanted that gold medal.

Four years later, remembered for his tragic failure on the ice, Dan Jansen appeared in the 1992 Games in Albertville, France. Jansen came prepared, well-trained, and focused. Despite his valiant effort to seek redemption, he again came up short, settling for fourth in the 500 and twenty-sixth in the 1000 meters.

Jansen exhibited his iron will to succeed but again failed to win a medal. He had trained diligently and shown himself worthy of being an Olympic contender but not an Olympic champion. Certainly he would have to admit that he was finished.

But this option did not sit well with Jansen. Tormented by his commitment to succeed, he was determined to try again. Like the apostle Paul, he pressed on toward the prize of his calling.

Two years later, at the 1994 Games in Norway, he returned to the Olympics for what would be his last opportunity to earn gold.

As the world watched, tension mounted. Many thought Jansen was either a glutton for punishment or a true hero. However, he knew he was genuinely capable. Once again on the world stage, victory would be incredible—defeat would be a terrible disappointment.

Jansen went out in the 500-meter event and again faltered. He came around a turn, lost his balance, and dragged his hand on the ice. He finished in eighth place. He had one more event—the 1000 meters.

What had to be going through his mind at this point? He had competed again and again, each time possessing the raw skills needed to win but each time falling victim to his emotions.

One more event—one more opportunity to bask in the glow of victory or walk away in the shadows of defeat.

Jansen went out in the 1000 at breakneck speed on a world-record pace. When he staggered once again, everyone in the crowd, and the millions of fans watching on television, shuddered to think of a replay of earlier events. But in a miraculous feat of athleticism, he was able to right himself, crossing the finish line in first place and setting a new world record in the process.

Jansen skated his victory lap carrying his baby daughter, Jane—named for his deceased sister. Tears spilled down his cheeks. The 10,000 cheering fans were riveted on this gutsy champion who had dared to come back time and again until he claimed his well-deserved prize. He had committed himself to one pursuit, and he had attained it.

High School

Whereas Dan Jansen was an overcomer and champion in the face of disappointment, I was a colossal failure in high school. I wish I could say that I went for the gold, but it simply isn't true.

(I can still hear my parents lamenting, "And he had so much potential!")

Like so many others, I wish I could turn the clock back and do it all over again. I look back at my high school days as wasted in many ways. I squandered the musical talents and athletic skills I had developed during childhood. I quit music lessons and dropped out of organized sports, committed to nothing and to no one in particular.

At the time, I did not recognize I was frittering my life away. As is often the case, only in retrospect did I gain clarity about this waste. Now I see how much I could have gained from and contributed to my high school experience. Now I can appreciate the consequences of my lack of commitment to anything or anyone.

Raised in a middle-class home, I wanted for nothing. I was not spoiled, but we had a nice life. I had a fine Christian background, established by firm and loving parents with strong moral fiber. Add to this a fairly athletic frame and reasonable intellectual skills. But I lacked clarity of vision when establishing goals. My expectations were too limited, much to the chagrin of my parents.

I recall vividly many discussions with my parents about my poor academic accomplishments.

"David, you can do so much better. Why don't you try harder?"

"I don't know," I would say. And I didn't know. I had no answer for them then and little more explanation now, other than some inherent fear of making a genuine commitment to excellence. I lacked the motivation to use my athletic and academic talents and settled for a life of pleasure. I was not committed to accomplishing great things, and my path and opportunities narrowed as a result. Any hopes for higher education would mean taking the less distinguished route through community college.

I regret my lack of vision and stunted dreams. I wonder if my limited expectations stifled a budding writer inside me. Was an explorer, historian, or journalist ready to blossom if had I been more committed to excellence?

Wanting More but Settling for Less

Chal and Cindy came to see me in a state of crisis. She was a petite, perky 23-year-old with short blond hair. She dressed smartly but with a hint of reserve. At times, she seemed to disappear behind her big blue eyes and shy demeanor.

Her boyfriend of one year, Chal, was much bolder, with a large moustache and curly brown hair sprouting from under his stained ball cap. He wore a Budweiser T-shirt and sported a rose tattoo on his forearm. He was stiff and distant, obviously uncomfortable.

I met with Chal and Cindy during an initial session to gather information about what had brought them to counseling. Cindy burst into tears almost immediately as she revealed she had caught Chal recently seeing an ex-girlfriend.

"I don't understand it at all," she cried. "We have a great relationship, and he says he loves me. But then he goes and sees Jessica. I feel like a total fool."

"What about it?" I asked Chal.

"It's true. I don't know why I do it, but I do. I can't seem to make a final decision between Cindy and Jessica. I have never lied to her about it."

Chal stared at me blankly, seemingly unmoved by Cindy's tears.

"I don't want to hurt her," Chal continued. "I do love her. But I'm confused."

I spent the balance of the session exploring their situation. They were in a crisis, and it was not a new story. Chal was caught between two women and seemed unable to decide on one or the other. In the meantime, he and Cindy struggled. I decided to see them individually to learn more about what might have brought them to this place in their relationship.

Chal had been raised in south Chicago, where poverty was rampant and crime was a way of life. Kids grew up in the city and usually stayed there, he said. He had barely graduated from high school.

Born to middle-class parents, he was raised in a family that was intact but plagued with alcoholism. His father liked to stop by the tavern after work and have a few beers with his buddies. However, the "few beers" often turned into more than a few, and he would stumble into the house well after Chal and his three siblings had gone to bed. Chal would wake up to his parents arguing over his father's drinking, and he would resolve never to be like his father. He resolved never to have a marriage like his parents had.

After high school Chal had the opportunity to move west. A couple of guys who lived in Washington state offered him a chance to come out and learn the electrical trade. He decided life couldn't be any worse than living in the housing developments of south Chicago, so he packed up and headed for Washington.

He met Cindy several months after he arrived—after he had already formed a relationship with Jessica. Everything appeared to be going well until Cindy found out that he had seen this ex-girlfriend, Jessica, on several occasions. After being caught, he openly admitted that he still had feelings for Jessica. And to make matters worse, she continued to pursue him. This broke Cindy's heart. She was trying to decide how much to tolerate.

"I used to go out with Jessica," Chal told me. "She's a lot of fun to be with, and I like her a lot. It seems like every time I'm ready to let her go and be exclusively with Cindy, Jessica gets ahold of me, and I can't say no. I know that it isn't fair to Cindy, and I've even told her to do what she has to do. I know how much this hurts her, and she has tried to pull away from me, but I don't want that. So I keep both of them hanging on. I know it's wrong, but I'm not sure what to do."

"Did you ever think this could happen to you when you first started dating?" I asked.

"I've always worried about my ability to commit to one person. And this situation just reinforces that concern. I like parts of Cindy as well as parts of Jessica. I can't seem to decide between them."

I asked Chal more about his upbringing. He shared how angry he had been at his parents—his father for his history of drinking and also for being gone so much; his mother for tolerating so much of this behavior. He wondered why his mother had stayed, but he rationalized her behavior as something she had done to survive because she had three children and no good way to support herself.

"I am curious about something, Chal," I said. "Do you think Cindy stays with you for similar reasons?"

"Well, I haven't thought about it. I don't know that I would stay as long as she has, that's for sure."

"That might be something worth considering. She might have self-esteem issues like your mother."

"Yes. In some ways she reminds me of my mother. My mom seemed to want so little for herself. If my parents could make it through the day and watch some television at night, that seemed like enough. I always knew I'd never settle for that kind of life, and so when the opportunity to move out here came, I jumped at it. But many of my dreams seem to be fading. I find myself settling for a way of life I never wanted. I find myself living from paycheck to paycheck, from one weekend to another weekend, and it bugs me. Cindy and Jessica are both a lot like me—big dreams but not much follow-through. They are ready to settle for things, just like I am. But I'm not really happy inside, and I'll bet they're not happy either."

As I listened to Chal's story, I realized he had learned to settle for limited expectations, at least partly in response to his parents, and this was impacting his ability to commit to one person. He had grown up in a world where each generation lived pretty much the same as the ones before. Chal was struggling to decide what his values were and what he wanted to do with his life. Although he wanted more for himself, he had much of his parents in him. It was as though he dared not dream too much. His ambivalence about expectations colored his relationships with Cindy and Jessica.

Lowering the Bar

When I talked with Cindy, she insisted she truly loved Chal even though her heart was breaking and her confidence waned. She watched as her two young daughters became more and more attached to him. Against her better judgment, she found herself caring more and more deeply for him even after finding out about his attraction to Jessica. He was a gentle man who had a strong spiritual faith. They enjoyed the same activities and goals. They had even talked about building a life together. She sensed that he loved her—in spite of being torn in his feelings about her and Jessica.

Cindy understood that she was placing herself in a precarious situation, and yet she loved Chal. Perhaps you have felt like this before. Her heart was stronger than her mind. She was completely focused on them being together in spite of the obvious obstacle.

As I listened to Cindy, I could see that she felt caught in a vicious circle. The more Chal pulled away, the more desperately she clung to him. As she clung to him, he became frustrated and lost respect for her. This was not the deciding factor leading him to see Jessica, but it did not help matters. All the while, Cindy's self-esteem was plummeting. The tears in her eyes told the story—she missed Chal and felt hopelessly entangled with him.

Cindy realized that she had somehow lowered the bar of her expectations. She felt exasperated with herself and wondered how she could have allowed herself to sink into such a situation. How could she settle for something that she knew would only cause her heartache?

"My friends think I'm nuts," Cindy said. "They say I should tell Chal, 'It's her or me.' They say I should stand up to him and tell him how it is. But that's a lot easier said than done. I love him, and he loves me. Walking away from a love like this isn't easy. I have even considered asking him to marry me to get away from her. I don't think people understand."

After meeting with both individually, I decided to see them again as a couple. I listened again to their story of one-sided commitment. I watched Cindy struggle with her feelings—anger at Chal and herself combined with intense sadness. As she cried, Chal watched and finally offered her a tissue.

"How do you feel when you see her hurting?" I asked.

"That's a stupid question," Chal answered. "It's not like I'm out to break hearts. I'm not a two-timing idiot."

"Yet you are seeing two women at the same time," I countered.

"But I'm not sneaking around on her. It's different," he said.

As I sat with Chal and Cindy, my heart also broke for them. They were a likeable, young couple with so many things going for them. They had a chance to become a healthy blended family. Both were caring people, except…

- Chal could not commit to her.
- Cindy kept naïvely hoping things would change.
- Cindy lowered her expectations.
- Chal lowered his expectations by seeing two women.

As I observed their dysfunctional dance, I reflected on the work of noted researcher and writer Pia Melody, author of *Facing Codependence*, who has written extensively on the topic of codependency. She notes three core symptoms associated with resentment and codependency.[1] Examining these may help us to understand why Cindy might lower the bar to include Chal and his unfaithfulness in her life.

Inappropriate Levels of Self-Esteem

Melody explains that if we believe a person has offended us, we experience a blow to our self-esteem, which causes shame about ourselves. This is because we feel we are being treated as if we have no worth and that perhaps we deserve such treatment.

Chal's actions were certainly a horrendous blow to Cindy's self-image. However, rather than responding in a reasonable way by setting healthy boundaries on his actions, she wallowed in her feelings of resentment toward Chal. She was angry and bitter toward him, imagining ways to punish both him and Jessica. She tried to compensate for her low self-esteem by directing her rage outwardly rather than tending to her wounds inwardly. This was all a result of her codependency.

Impaired Boundaries

If we have established no firm boundaries, we may be especially offended because we feel powerless to stop the assault. When we feel anger, fear, and pain, we also feel resentment. We want other people to change their behavior when the real key is changing our own.

I could see the lack of boundaries with Cindy. She seemed helpless to stand up to Chal. Even though she told him how angry she was about his behavior, she did not set healthy boundaries that would protect her from being hurt in the future.

Melody says that even when we set boundaries, people more powerful than ourselves—such as Chal—may still transgress them. But living with resentment is different from feeling pain and anger, both of which are necessary for recovery. Resentment keeps us stuck in rehearsing our wounds; we can use anger to make important changes in our lives.

Difficulty Owning Reality

Melody identifies three ways this symptom can contribute to resentment. One is when we experience inaccurate or skewed thinking—this did not seem to be the case with Cindy. She knew that she was tolerating inappropriate behavior. She knew she was settling for too little in her life, and she was embarrassed by it.

A second is having difficulty figuring out what we think and feel and being unable to fully acknowledge the impact of another's behavior on us. We may be able to feel pain, fear, or anger about our perception of being wronged, but we may be less able to recognize it or express it in a healthy way. This was certainly true of Cindy, who tended to erupt with outbursts of rage when she found out Chal had seen Jessica again even though she knew that it would happen sooner or later.

The third way this occurs is when we can't "own" our thinking about ourselves. Instead, we use the opinion others have of us to define ourselves. When other people don't think about us the way we think they should, we feel resentment. Cindy was experiencing some of this because she was aware that Chal looked down on her in some ways for tolerating his inappropriate behavior.

As a result of her codependency, Cindy lowered her standards and settled for far less than she wanted. She hated herself for doing so and desperately wanted to be stronger. She wanted to be assertive and set healthier boundaries. She knew that these steps would help her to be happier and perhaps even save their relationship. But translating what we know to be right into action can be very difficult.

Split Personality

Chal struggled with lowering the bar and symptoms of codependency as well. He could see how these issues affected his personality. Different parts of him wanted different things. Although he had vowed to stay away from alcohol because of the damage it caused his father and his parents' marriage, he still stopped by the bar for drinks with the guys occasionally. Although he believed in fidelity to one person, he was attracted to two women, both of whom were willing to take the parts he was willing to offer. He felt as if he were splitting apart inside.

Chal was at war with himself, and his struggles with the two women only made his inner conflict more severe. He was ready to make a name for himself in the electrical field, yet he was mired in a sea of ambivalence. He could feel the downward pull, coaxing him to settle for things he didn't want to settle for. He could feel the temptation to simply work nine to five as a mediocre electrician rather than accepting opportunities to work harder to be truly successful. He partly felt that dream was far too lofty for a boy from south Chicago and would only lead to disappointment.

His parents had made it clear that their family was working class. They lived a solid life but never expected too much. Chal had watched his father work hard as a pressman in the newspaper industry. He was proud of his accomplishments and had even suggested Chal join him there. But Chal wanted to carve out his own path. He had secretly held out for the possibility that he might make a fortune in real estate while also acknowledging that this was probably a pipe dream. Still, the dream never completely died, and he told me that he still thought about buying some property, developing it, and selling it. He was torn in his dreams for a mate and his dreams for a career.

The Smallness of Fear

As we consider Chal's unwillingness to commit, we must keep the issue of fear in our minds. Fear, more than any other emotion, limits our options. Fear keeps our world small. It limits our perspective, narrows our vision, and reduces our ability to commit.

Looking back at my reluctance to commit myself to anything or anyone during my high school years, I suspect that fear was the underlying cause. I played it safe—or perhaps I did not feel safe enough to truly test my capabilities. Consider this acronym:

F—false
E—evidence
A—appearing
R—real

You have undoubtedly discovered that your own fear is rarely based upon reality. Men who fear commitment often base their feelings on something that happened in another time, probably involving another person. Regardless, the emotion *feels* real and certainly limits their options.

Scott Peck, in *The Road Less Traveled,* says problems related to commitment are an inherent part of most psychiatric disorders. He states that character-disordered people tend to make only shallow commitments because they do not understand what commitment is all about. "Because their parents failed to commit themselves to them as children in any meaningful way, they grew up without the experience of commitment."

Neurotics—folks like Chal and Cindy—understand the notion of commitment but may be paralyzed by the fear of it. Chal wouldn't make the decision between two women; Cindy feared making the decision to set healthy boundaries on Chal. Peck's words hit home:

> Usually their experience of early childhood was one in which their parents were sufficiently committed to them for them to form a commitment to their parents in return. Subsequently, however, a cessation of parental love through death, abandonment or chronic rejection, has the effect of making the child's unrequited commitment an experience of intolerable pain. New commitments, then, are naturally dreaded. Such injuries can be healed only if it is possible for the

person to have a basic and more satisfying experience with commitment at a later date.[2]

Fear shuts us down. Fear causes us to close our heart. Dean Ornish, in his book *Love and Survival,* says this:

> It is particularly difficult for us to develop intimate and loving relationships if we grew up in a family in which intimacy was dangerous because of emotional, physical, or sexual abuse. The heart develops a particularly strong armor to protect and defend itself, but the same emotional defenses that protect us can also isolate us if they always remain up, if nowhere and no one feels safe enough to let down our walls. When I use the term "opening your heart" I mean your willingness to allow yourself to be open and vulnerable to another person. We can only be intimate to the degree that we are willing to be open and vulnerable.[3]

The apostle James describes the way fear undermines commitment. Listen to his counsel translated from the pen of Eugene Peterson, author of The Message: "People who 'worry their prayers' are like wind-whipped waves. Don't think you're going to get anything from the Master that way, adrift at sea, keeping all your options open" (James 1:6-8).

As James tells us, those who try to keep their options open are often consumed by worry. They don't believe that God has their best welfare in mind, so they don't have the confidence to move forward confidently.

Another translation of this verse provides a very apt description of the person who cannot commit. "For he that wavereth is like a wave of the sea driven with the wind and tossed; he is troubled, restless, unquiet, and impatient; and he is fickle, inconstant, unstable, and unsettled; and is easily carried away with every wind of doctrine, temptation and lust."[4]

Perhaps you have experienced a situation like this. You sensed your man was wavering. You knew he was fearful even though he may have denied it. You could feel the restlessness in his spirit. Like Chal, your man may be wavering between you and someone else. He may be torn between you and another focus in his life. If he is wavering, the culprit is probably fear.

The Magnitude of Commitment

If fear causes smallness—a constriction of vision and a tendency to cling to any vestiges of self-esteem you have—commitment often causes your vision to expand. When you set your sights on something, when you commit to it, when you act in accordance with your beliefs, that goal becomes larger in your mind. When you set your sights on *someone*, when you commit to a person, he or she also becomes larger, expanded in your life.

Consider the life of Christ. He committed Himself to a course of action, knowing the outcome. He knew Judas would betray Him, Peter would deny Him, and His disciples would discourage Him in the Garden of Gethsemane. He knew that even after countless miracles and hours of teaching His disciples, they would still not understand Him. Yet despite the cost, He bet everything on this ragtag band of men and even built what was to become His church upon them. And the rest is history. The Christian faith has spread across continents and continues to change millions of lives each day. Jesus' commitment to His mission and to His men transformed the world.

In my work with Chal, we examined his inherent fear of commitment. We explored his "wind-whipped" frame of mind and how keeping his options open actually restricted his life. We saw that his ambivalence could cost him both women.

Chal initially denied being afraid. He denied that he was making his world small by keeping his options open. In fact, as he saw it, he was enlarging his world. But he admitted that in the process he was not being completely honest with Cindy or

Jessica, nor was he being completely honest with himself. Only in time did he realize that fear was keeping his world smaller than it needed to be.

Gradually, Chal came to see and feel the power and depth that accompany commitment. Ultimately, he decided to take the risk—and yes, there is always a risk—in committing to Cindy. He told Jessica not to contact him in the future, closing the door tightly on that possible relationship. Cindy helped him in this process by setting healthy boundaries and expecting more from her relationships.

Cindy had to make some tough decisions and ultimatums. She informed Chal that should he decide again to pursue Jessica, it would be without her in his life. The boundary was clear. The choice would be his to make.

At this time, both Cindy and Chal are enjoying the fruits of living in the expansion of commitment. They have dedicated themselves to making this relationship be all that it can possibly be, talking more honestly about marriage as well. They agree that a committed relationship is the best place to let their hair down, to learn about each other completely, and to set about the task of loving each other as fully as possible.

As I worked with Chal and Cindy, now with the added luxury of their commitment to one another, we were able to talk about sharing emotional intimacies with one another. Without commitment, complete emotional honesty is impossible. Why would anyone share the depths of his or her heart and soul with someone who may be gone tomorrow? Of course, this makes no sense. But with a commitment to re-create their relationship, Chal and Cindy were able to expand the horizons of their emotional life.

They were now ready to commit to what Daphne Rose Kingma calls "emotional bravery." In *The Book of Love*, Kingma says, "Most of us are emotional chickens, afraid to communicate what we're feeling, afraid that what we disclose will be ignored, made fun of, or ridiculed." She challenges us to practice several things.

Whenever you're having the slightest unsettled feeling that comes from not saying what's on your mind, try asking yourself...

- *What it is that I'm not saying?*
- *Why am I not saying it right now?*[5]

Kingma tells us the truth. When we are committed to one another and to sharing what is on our minds, our relationships will improve because they will contain more of the truth of who we really are.

Chal, Cindy, and I also explored the topic of spiritual intimacy—that some obligations come with serving Christ. We discussed the importance of treating one another with the respect that a child of God deserves—with complete fidelity. Chal was now committed to treating Cindy with that respect, and Cindy was also determined to treat herself with the respect she deserved. Cindy is willing to let Chal go if he will not honor her with faithfulness. We reviewed together Scriptures about honoring one another, such as treating each other as temples of the Holy Spirit (1 Corinthians 6:19).

Chal and Cindy are working at understanding and applying their Christian faith to their relationship. They see their relationship as an opportunity to commit themselves to one another and to Christ. They realize that partial commitments are ineffective.

Making It Safe for the Man in Your Life

Fear constricts a man's heart and makes him want to run. Conversely, safety will help him open his heart, creating a place for love. But how do you make him feel safe? Dr. George Weinberg, in his wonderful book *Why Men Won't Commit*, offers us many important insights into this question.

Before offering several important truths that will help you in your relationship with your man, let me offer an observation Dr. Weinberg and many others have made. Weinberg states emphatically that men are not as strong as they appear. "He doesn't hold all the cards. He is just pretending to. If you can realize the truth, that men are the weaker sex, you will have ten times the chance in your relationship. The man in your life isn't nearly as strong as he looks."[6]

Weinberg goes on to give additional advice about men's needs, especially as they pertain to the issue of safety. He says your man has four basic needs, and these determine his gut reaction to you at every stage of a relationship.

First, *he needs to be recognized as special.* I suspect that you already knew that. If you have been in a relationship with a man for more than five minutes, you know that his ego must be stroked, or he may start pouting, sulking, or displaying some other inappropriate reaction.

A man needs to be appreciated not just as a man but also in a personal way. He needs to know he is a distinct individual to you, not like other men you may have met.

Second, *he needs to travel light.* Weinberg says this springs from a fear of being encumbered.

> You may have a little of this need yourself, but you probably aren't nearly as paranoid as most men are about being limited or tied down…A serious fear of his is that commitment will require him to surrender all his "hard-won" masculine freedoms. He needs to understand that committing to you does not mean emasculation or imprisonment. You can reassure him that it's safe to move forward with you, and that, even with marriage and a family, he can still travel light and be free—within reason, of course.[7]

Third, *he needs loyalty.* Weinberg says that men are often more afraid of being betrayed than women are. Men have to be in control at all times to prove their masculinity. The idea of "his woman" not being completely on his side unmans him.

Fourth, *he needs to be close emotionally.* Weinberg says, and I concur, that men have a need for closeness just as you do. However, a man feels conflicted about this because a desire for closeness does not make him feel more like a man. So he finds it hard, if not impossible, to say that he wants to be close. Although he thirsts for this intimacy, he often may do little to create it. At the same time, he may be resentful when it is not there. Sound familiar?

Knowing these facts about your man will empower you to know how to interact with him and, more importantly, how to make him feel safe enough to come close and commit to you.

Raising the Bar

When the going gets rough, we sometimes tend to lose sight of our objectives and lower the bar that establishes what we will accept in our lives. This certainly happens in relationships—our vision narrows, we limit possibilities, and the outcome is dissatisfaction for all involved. When we lower our standards, when we accept anything less than a committed relationship, we cheat ourselves.

Instead of lowering the bar, we need to raise it. We need to make an unswerving commitment to our mate and not look back. In this environment of love and safety, we will experience the possibility of emotional transparency.

Chal increased the possibilities in his life by making a commitment to Cindy, and she simultaneously raised the bar on what she would tolerate. She practiced the art of assertiveness, treating herself as the prized child of God that she is, recognizing that she has worth regardless of Chal's actions. The result was positive. As she set firmer boundaries, Chal responded by expanding his world with a commitment to her.

Certainly no one would question the premise that love flourishes in an environment of commitment and safety. When we lower the bar, when we strive for anything less than the gold in our relationships and live in fear, we choke off the possibilities of love.

For love to flourish, you will need to make a commitment to your mate and demand a commitment in return as well. Go ahead. Take the risk. Raise the bar for yourself and your mate and see what happens. You'll be glad you did.

THREE

COME CLOSE, GET AWAY

*All changes, even the most longed for, have their melancholy;
for what we leave behind us is a part of ourselves; we must
die to one life before we can enter another.*

ANATOLE FRANCE

Looking out from the comfort of my motel room, I watched excitedly as snowflakes danced in the morning sky, landing tenderly on the trees and creating a winter wonderland. I hadn't seen snow for months, having left 60-degree weather back in Washington. I cherished each moment because I would be leaving frosty New York and flying back home later that afternoon. I didn't even consider that the weather might foul my plans.

The storm brought an end to a wonderful two-day retreat for me and an exquisite interview process for my youngest son, Tyson, at New York Medical College, where his older brother,

Josh, already attends school. Grandparents, parents, and friends prayed for Tyson's admission, and there were many small indications that God was doing some nice work on his behalf.

Undaunted by the snow and wind, my two intrepid sons decided we could still fit in a trip to a local coffee shop before heading to John F. Kennedy Airport, where Tyson and I would catch a flight to Seattle. Our plans were abruptly altered when we hit the parkway. Lights flashed ahead as our car crawled forward, passing not one but two fender-benders in the snowstorm. We inched along for the next hour, gaining perhaps a quarter mile of ground. At this rate we would be at the airport three hours late. It was time for a new plan.

We reluctantly scuttled our coffee mission and headed for the train station, where Ty and I said goodbye to Josh, hoping the train could get us to the airport. We knew we would not get to the airport on time. All we could do was hope the flight would be delayed due to inclement weather. After getting on the train, which was crowded with cold, unsettled travelers, we were informed by airline personnel that the flight had been cancelled.

My mind raced with possibilities about how to get back to my counseling practice the next day. My schedule was filled with clients. However, the airline had other plans...or rather, no plans. When we arrived at the airport, a maelstrom of activity met us. Like ants in a dustbowl after their home has been destroyed, people scurried about in hapless, frenetic commotion. No one seemed to be in charge; no one was able to help get my son and me back home. And no one was able to calm my frayed nerves.

Having never been in a situation like this before, I did not handle it well. It was getting late, and hopes for getting home that night were dim. Unsympathetic, grumpy airline workers told us that our chances of getting home the next night were negligible as well because the seats had all been sold. I thought we should have been given priority for those seats because our flight had been canceled, but that's not how it works. No flight home, no hotel rooms available, no restaurants open, no hope. We joined the throngs of other weary travelers with makeshift beds on the floor.

Tired, hungry, and irritable, Tyson and I became testy with one another. He scolded me for my intolerance, which I found to be intolerant on his part. I wanted to end our day together feeling close and grateful, to bask together in the afterglow of his wonderful interview, but I was annoyed with anyone, including him, who had anything other than good news for me. In hindsight, he was probably acting more mature in that situation than his father.

It was now very late, and no one had been able to help. We would be spending the night on the floor along with hundreds of other cranky travelers. The building was cold, the floor was hard, and we were exhausted and very irritable. We camped for the night in the most haphazard version of a tent city I have ever seen. People curled up in blue airline-blanketed balls in every corner, futilely trying to get some rest. Cell phones rang every few seconds, and people grumbled as they made frantic efforts to get out of New York and back home to loved ones. But no one was having any luck. We were all stuck, harboring only a vague hope that the next day might bring better weather and relief.

I spent the night desperate for a shower and warm bed but having to settle for a thin blanket on a cold hard floor next to a fake potted plant. I wanted to be comforted in my distress, and yet I wanted everyone to get away from me. My tank was empty, and I had nothing left to give. Depleted, exhausted, frightened of being stuck in an unfamiliar airport, and irritable, I was not a good traveling companion.

Tyson and I have since talked about this fateful evening in New York, agreeing that we must learn to expect the unexpected—to roll with the punches. I apologized for my short temper and irritability. We agreed to ask for what we need, not being afraid to be vulnerable with one another.

A Pattern of Bad Choices

Like me at JFK, Caroline did not make the best "traveling companion." Her relational journeys typically ended badly, in large part because her choices of partners were poor. Her life was filled with petulance, fatigue, and apprehension—from many sources. Her pattern was to get close to others and then push them away or be abandoned. She could sustain relationships for short times, but then she would falter, as would her partners. This was the mosaic of her troubled life.

Caroline did not volunteer to see me. She had been required to participate in a psychological evaluation to assess her abilities to parent her three young children, who had been removed three months earlier from her care for failing to protect them. The reports said that Caroline failed to maintain a healthy living situation for her children. This was part of the assessment:

"Caroline is a bright, young woman who has the ability to be a better mother than she has been. She moves from relationship to relationship, all with men who treat her badly. There are signs of domestic violence, and the kids show emotional problems. Children were removed after being seen unsupervised again in the housing development."

I glanced again at the report while looking at Caroline, a sad, haggard young woman who appeared older than her 24 years. She was dour in her presentation, making no effort to impress me—even with custody of her children on the line. Chipped fingernail polish, tobacco-stained fingers, a tattooed cross in the flesh next to her thumb, and attire that included an old sweatshirt and jeans indicated to me that she had packed a lot of living into her short life.

Caroline sat near me in my office, fumbling with a pen. She clutched a clipboard that held papers I'd asked her to complete.

In spite of her rumpled appearance, I soon realized she was bright and articulate. At first, she offered little information and was immediately defensive. She told me the authorities removed her children for no reason, and she wondered what she would have to do to get them back. But before long, her anger gave way to sadness. She began to weep as she talked about losing her children.

"I don't suppose you've ever had your kids taken away," she said angrily. Before I could answer she returned to venting her feelings. "No, I didn't think so." She dabbed at her eyes. "All I'm guilty of is stringing together a series of bad men. That's my crime. And for that I lose my kids. Does that make sense to you?"

"Well, Caroline, that depends. On the surface it might not make sense. But maybe together we can figure out why the state is concerned about your parenting. They must have some reason for doing this. And I'm guessing that you have a pretty good idea what it is."

Caroline laid her pen and clipboard deliberately on the table, then leaned toward me. She braced herself as if she needed support to tell me her story.

"You know, I always thought I'd be more than this. Then the kids came, and it's been hand-to-mouth. I've been on welfare ever since, unable to go to college as I planned. I jump from relationship to relationship, and all I get is another kid."

"You sound pretty discouraged," I offered.

"Look, I have nothing but bad luck with men. The kids' fathers took off because they couldn't handle the responsibility. The other men I've been with were nice for a while—then they disappeared. They had about as much commitment to me and the kids as I have to that old pickup out front. I wasn't enough of something for them. I'm not sure what they were looking for, but it wasn't me. It wasn't the kids."

"We should talk more about that, Caroline," I said. "But first I'd like to know why the state stepped in. What led up to the kids being taken?"

"The state takes kids all the time. It's a game they play. I know mothers who are a lot worse than I am, and they still have their kids."

"I doubt that the state wants your children, Caroline. In fact, I know they don't. They've asked me to tell them what it might take to get the kids back home with you. That's the angle I want to pursue. I'd like to know whether you think your problems with men have impacted your kids."

Caroline bristled at first, but then she gradually softened. Just when she appeared ready to attack me, she broke down and started crying again. She was too tired to fight any longer.

"Yeah, I hear you. A month ago you would have seen a lot of venom coming out of me. Lots of blame and hurt. Today, just a lot of hurt. And a lot of regret. I can see their point. I can see why they would not want the children to be around the men I've chosen. I've been thinking about how I choose the men in my life and about what I can do to protect my kids in the future. It's not the state's fault, and I'm not going to blame them anymore."

"I'll bet accepting that is easier said than done, especially with your kids gone. Owning up to our part of problems is hard for any of us, but that is the only way things can ever change."

"Yes, and I want to change things. I'm tired of being attracted to 'bad boys' or those who need mothers. I'm tired of these guys pulling me away from being a healthy parent to my kids. I want to find a man who can be committed to me and the kids and who can be a man in every sense of the word. I'm ready for that."

"I hear you, Caroline," I said. "I think you are certainly more ready now than before, but you may still have some work to do before that can happen. You may need to look back even more carefully at your patterns so that you can really understand why you are attracted to emotionally immature men."

We agreed to review her past behaviors, with the understanding that she might want to work on these issues in counseling after her evaluation was complete.

With that, Caroline began to share her history.

She was first married at age 19 to Jake, the father of her oldest child. She had known Jake since high school. He was a trouble-maker, but they had fun together. They married after high school, but the relationship didn't last due to his alcohol and drug abuse. He rarely worked, leaving her to carry the financial load with her part-time work as a waitress, adding tension to their marriage as well. She finally left him after he cheated on her.

She jumped into another relationship without waiting. She met Tim through mutual friends. Tim had shown interest in her, and she wanted to be in a relationship. They started living together almost immediately, and they had a child within two years. Although Tim was a bit more stable than Jake, they used drugs together, and Tim ultimately decided he didn't want to be in a relationship. She remains angry with Tim even now for his refusal to pay child support.

Caroline said that after Tim she "swore off men for a while." For her, this apparently meant several months. Before long, however, she was involved with the drummer of a band passing through town. She traveled with the band for a while, becoming pregnant again. She embarrassingly said this was her third pregnancy from three different men. "The traveling got old, and I left Jack because of the lifestyle. It was not good for me or the kids."

"I am in another relationship now. It has its ups and downs. Darren is working but not at the best job. We have been together for six months. We are both clean and sober and are going to church. I think we have a chance, but we have to keep working our programs and going to counseling. I want the kids back, and I know that I have to learn to have healthy relationships. I have to learn how to really be in a relationship and how to expect that from the man I am with. I need to make sure that my man is able to be stable, committed, caring, and sensitive to me and the kids. I think it can happen, but it will take some work."

Caroline and I explored her patterns, which were obvious when she stood back and looked at them objectively without anger or naïveté clouding her perceptions. She noticed several things about the men she became involved with. Perhaps this is the pattern for the men who have been part of your history as well:

- They were all immature, taking far more than they gave to the relationship.
- They had severe emotional problems.
- Most had drug and alcohol issues.
- Most had a speckled work history.
- Most had a limited ability to commit to relationships.
- Most had instability in their early family life.

After listening to Caroline share her concerns, which were remarkably accurate, I explained to her my simple way of assessing people.

A Pyramid of Maturity

I have worked with many Carolines over the years. I evaluate and counsel countless women who have repeatedly been involved with men with troubling pasts.

Mary Ellen Donovan and William Ryan, in their book *Love Blocks,* say that people like Caroline and the men in her life can take love from others but only on a short-term basis.

> They may be able to connect very intimately with a partner, friend, or family member in the now, but they can't be counted on to be around five months or five years from now. Although they might want very much to promise loved ones that they'll be there for them always and forever, there's something operating within

their psyches that makes it impossible or at least very difficult.[1]

I have helped many people come to understand their patterns and change them. One of the first things I do is offer them a simple way of understanding their choices. This is a beginning step toward change. I ask them to rate their choices using my "baseball pyramid," which provides a simple way of thinking about our choices in relationships.

I draw a pyramid with four levels, labeled like this:

Peewee leaguers are on the lowest level. These people are…

- immature
- emotionally underdeveloped
- often involved with drugs, alcohol, or other addictions
- usually incapable of being in a committed relationship by virtue of their addictions and subsequent immaturity
- because of their immense problems, they do not have a "self" to bring to the relationship

Minor leaguers are no longer practicing their addiction, but they are not working through any kind of recovery program. Therefore, these people…

- are in a "dry drunk" state
- have all the character traits of people who are addicted or dysfunctional
- do not have well-developed communication or conflict resolution skills
- are not in touch with their feelings
- do not know how to have a healthy, committed relationship

Major leaguers are those few who have "done their work." These people…

- have either been in some kind of recovery process, counseling, or both
- recognize their need for deeper spiritual and psychological tools
- humbly tell you that they do not have all the answers and are willing to seek them
- have been in healthy relationships, and though they may have failed in some, they have learned from them
- are free from serious addiction or dysfunctional patterns and are ready for a committed relationship

All-stars are those you truly are looking for. The catch is this—you have to be one yourself before you can attract one because we tend to be attracted to people in our own league. These select people are...

- mature
- responsible
- spiritually sensitive
- ready for a committed relationship

When I show women this chart, their eyes open wide. They now have a visual outline for the choices they have made. They realize, quickly, that they have played in a league that can only lead to trouble for them. This insight alone is not enough to change things for them, but it is a beginning. They are able to see where they have been playing and how they might begin to change things.

When I showed Caroline this chart, she nodded with understanding. When I asked her what league she had played in, she quickly pointed to the peewee leaguers. When I asked her where she wanted to play, she said, "All-stars." She smiled as we agreed she was capable of making necessary changes—but they would begin with her.

Motivations

Like many women I counsel, Caroline had little understanding of why she chose certain men. People are often puzzled about their destructive decisions because they don't understand their motivations and other obvious factors that could help them make better judgments. People must realize and accept several truths about their choices. Some are obvious; others are less so.

First, *people make choices about whom they want to be involved with.* Yes, this may sound obvious, but many—in fact, far too many—like to ascribe their motives and choices to others. They fall back on excuses: "I couldn't help myself," "They chose me; I didn't choose them," "I didn't know what I was doing," or "The wrong people are attracted to me."

Perhaps you see yourself thinking this way at times. You find yourself in a troubled situation and want to blame it on something or someone else. The first step toward making better choices is to own your responsibility in your decisions.

Second, *people are often surprised about the people they have chosen to be involved with.* Because motivations are sometimes veiled by the subconscious, we may be surprised to find ourselves in the relationships we are in. Few people move into relationships fully aware of why they are attracted to their partners. They are often truly surprised when they find themselves in a destructive relationship. This is because they have not taken the time to fully examine their motivations and actions.

Third, *people pick others to be involved with based upon their own likes and dislikes as well as common levels of self-esteem.* This is characterized in the old proverb "Birds of a feather flock together." It is true. We hang around with people who will accept us and who see the world the same way we do. We seek those with like values and views. For that reason, if you are surprised by the kind of people you attract, the first thing to do is look in the mirror.

Finally, *you can become much smarter about the relationships in which you get involved.* You can learn more about personality makeup and the types of people that are good for you—and the types that are not. You can understand old, unfinished business in your life, including self-esteem issues and destructive character traits that are likely to create havoc in your relationships. Ask yourself the following questions:

- Do you have a history of destructive partners, marriages, or relationships?
- Have you taken the time to understand your patterns?
- What are the patterns? Do you attract distant, uncaring men?
- Suffocating, needy men?
- Spiritually immature men?
- Men who are unable to commit?

Wounded Men

People with the problems I have described are obviously wounded. Men who ruin their lives with alcohol, drugs, pornography, or any number of other addictions have a hole in their soul. They frantically try to fill it with something, anything, that makes them feel better temporarily. Their world is dictated by immediate pleasure, and they cannot be concerned with long-range (committed) thinking.

Let me offer you a brief picture of the addicted or dysfunctional person. Perhaps you have been there and will recognize some of these symptoms. Or perhaps you have been involved with someone who has been caught in the downward spiral of alcoholism or drug addiction. Perhaps you have been married to a man desperately attached to the slipperiness of worldly success and workaholism. When you examine the traits common to addicted people, consider how they have lost their "self" and why they cannot possibly be successful in a committed relationship—they simply have no self to bring to the relationship.

False self: Addicted or dysfunctional people spend a lot of time erecting a false self. They construct zones of protection all around them, ensuring that no one really gets to know them. They build thick walls of security and deception, and they invest a tremendous amount of energy reinforcing them. They are so busy trying to impress others that they do not know how to be real. They are so busy playing a part—this false self they have created—that they don't understand what is important to them other than indulging their addiction.

Neglecting their own needs: Having spent energy living with the false self, addicted or dysfunctional people have invested no real time in attending to their own needs. They have lost sight of their own spiritual and emotional development. They are truly lost and do not even know it. Often they are spiritually, emotionally, and physically malnourished.

Low self-esteem: Not surprisingly, these individuals feel badly about themselves. At some level, they know that they are phonies. They realize they have cheated and hurt others as well as themselves, and they feel guilty about that. They live in regret because they have not been able to sustain healthy relationships and are deeply lonely.

Loss of control: They desperately strive to be in charge, but their world is spiraling out of control. They have destroyed—or are on the verge of destroying—their relationships, are often in financial ruin, and have lost much of what is important to them.

Loss of feelings: Addicted or dysfunctional people do not know what they are feeling. They are in pain and know that they hurt, but they are not able to recognize and articulate their feelings. This central aspect of relating is not available to them.

Distrust: Addicted or dysfunctional people are often paranoid and distrusting. Because they are caught up in a world of deceit, they cannot safely share their inner life with others. This is a big part of the reason they cannot come close for any significant length of time.

Fear of abandonment: Even while addicted or dysfunctional people are unable to be committed to others, they fear abandonment. They push others away but fear being alone. They live in a desperate and painfully forlorn world.

Difficulty giving and receiving love: Addicted or dysfunctional people are unable to give and receive love. They have not invested the time or energy to learn the nuances of creating a loving relationship. In fact, they cannot perform many of the mini-tasks associated with giving love.

Caroline sought love from a series of wounded, dysfunctional men. She sought water from empty wells and yet did not realize it. Each time she went to the well she undoubtedly thought she would find water, but we could have easily predicted that she would be disappointed again and again and again. She sought love, affection, and attention from men who were only able to give it for small periods of time because they had no healthy self from which to give.

We have discussed Caroline's choice of men. But what about her ability to give and receive love? What of her ability to trust, nurture, and nourish a relationship? Was she any better off than those to whom she went for a loving relationship? No. Clearly we can see that Caroline set herself up to be in a relationship lacking commitment, for she herself had a limited sense of self to give to others. Caroline had been wounded earlier in her life by a troubled family filled with violence and instability. Burdened by these unresolved issues, she repeated old family patterns and felt safe playing in a small and demeaning league. She was attracted to men who were similar to her in many ways.

Deep down, Caroline knows that until she radically changes, she will simply continue to make the same mistakes. She is beginning to see her patterns in choosing men and how they relate to her own self-esteem. She will end up with men who can only offer her a facsimile of the real thing for a very limited period of time.

These men will disappear, disappoint, and leave her as empty as when she started the relationship.

And so her task, and perhaps yours as well, is to create a strong sense of self by building the emotional and spiritual maturity we must have to move and breathe in a healthy manner. From this place, she will be able to make better choices and will gravitate toward the well that provides nourishing, living water.

Emotional and Spiritual Maturity

Lives of physical, spiritual, and emotional abuse—as well as substance abuse—leave our psyche devastated. Abuse and the trauma that accompanies it render us incapable of sustaining even the most meager relationships. They leave us with holes in our psyche and our soul, which we constantly try to repair with fillers. Developing a whole self and learning to form healthy, committed, and emotionally vulnerable relationships will lead to emotional and spiritual maturity. Let's consider what this means.

Certainly we would all agree that someone can be 30 years old chronologically and 20 years old emotionally. Abuse or emotional problems may have stifled that person's emotional development.

The story is told of a veteran schoolteacher who was looking forward to a promotion. She had taught for many years and had seniority. However, the promotion went to a teacher with less seniority, and she was upset.

"How can you do this to me?" she asked her vice principal. "I've been teaching for 30 years!"

"Unfortunately," he replied calmly, "you've been teaching one year 30 times."

Sadly, many of us have been marking time. We have grown older physically while remaining stifled emotionally. Many who have spent years mired in addictions have not learned or grown from their experiences. They are 20-year-olds in 50-year-old bodies.

Let's consider some symptoms of emotional immaturity, taken from the writings of Dr. Jerome Murray. Reflect on where you and your partner are in relation to these traits. Consider the effect of these traits on commitment and transparency.

1. *Volatile emotions:* Emotional volatility includes such things as explosive behavior, temper tantrums, low frustration tolerance, responses out of proportion to the cause, oversensitivity, inability to take criticism, unreasonable jealousy, unwillingness to forgive, and capricious fluctuation in moods.

2. *Overdependence:* Some people rely on others when they should be self-reliant, or they allow an appropriate dependence to last too long. This includes being easily influenced, indecisive, and prone to snap judgments. Overly dependent people fear change, preferring accustomed situations and behavior to the uncertainty of change and the challenge of adjustment.

3. *Stimulation hunger:* This includes demanding immediate attention or gratification and being unable to wait for anything. Stimulation-hungry people are incapable of putting off present desires in order to gain a future reward.

4. *Egocentricity:* Egocentricity is self-centeredness. Its major manifestation is selfishness associated with low self-esteem. Self-centered people have no regard for others, and they have only slight regard for themselves. An egocentric person is preoccupied with his or her own feelings and symptoms.

Now let's consider the traits of the emotionally mature individual.

1. *The ability to give and receive love:* Emotional maturity fosters a sense of security that permits vulnerability. A

mature person can show his vulnerability by expressing love and accepting expressions of love from others.

2. *The ability to face reality and deal with it:* Mature people do not avoid confrontations with reality. They process overdue bills, interpersonal problems, and other difficulties that demand character and integrity.

3. *An interest in giving and receiving:* Mature people possess a sense of personal security that permits them to consider the needs of others and give their own money, time, or effort to enhance the quality of life of those they love.

4. *The capacity to relate positively to life experience:* Mature people view life experiences as learning opportunities, and when they are positive they enjoy them and revel in life. When the experiences are negative, they accept personal responsibility and are confident they can learn from them and improve life.

5. *The ability to learn from experience:* When people can learn from experience, they can face reality and relate positively to life experiences. Immature people do not learn from positive or negative experiences.

6. *The ability to accept frustration:* When things don't go as anticipated, immature people stamp their feet, hold their breath, and bemoan their fate. Conversely, mature people consider using another approach or going in another direction and moving on with their life.

7. *The ability to handle hostility constructively:* When frustrated, the immature person looks for someone to blame. The mature person looks for a solution. Immature people attack people; mature people attack problems.

8. *Relative freedom from tension:* Mature people generally feel loved, and their approach to life imbues them with

a relaxed confidence in their ability to get what they want and need.[2]

This list highlights the relevance of emotional maturity to stable, healthy, and committed relationships. Without a modicum of these qualities, your relationship will feel like a boat without a rudder. You may experience plenty of highs, but there will be many lows, and a healthy relational commitment will likely elude you.

But emotional maturity is only one of the twin treasures you need on this journey of healthy relating. The other is spiritual maturity. Some consider spiritual maturity to refer to the relationships we have with our self, others, and the universe. But I consider it to entail much more than that.

George Gallup and Timothy Jones, in their book *The Saints Among Us*, define spiritual maturity as a genuine encounter with God that will change us permanently and unavoidably. They suggest that spiritual maturity does not just happen and that we must cultivate lives of prayer and spiritual discipline.

Billy Graham popularized the term "born again" to describe people coming to a vibrant faith. This certainly is not only a one-time event but also a process for someone who grows into "the measure of the stature of the fullness of Christ" (Ephesians 4:13 NKJV). James talks about spiritual maturity this way:

> Consider it pure joy, my brothers, whenever you face trials of many kinds, because you know that the testing of your faith develops perseverance. Perseverance must finish its work so that you may be mature and complete, not lacking anything (James 1:2-4).

In their studies, Gallup and Jones list nine qualities that characterize mature Christians. People who possess these qualities are better equipped to be in healthy, committed relationships.

1. *Prayer:* They set aside time every day to commune with God through prayer. It isn't a haphazard affair.

2. *Presence:* God is no stranger. He is actively present.

3. *Power:* Spiritually mature people have experienced the power of God. They do not doubt that God lives and acts.

4. *Happiness:* They regard themselves as happier than the population in general. Their faith sustains them.

5. *Humility:* They do not take themselves too seriously or sell themselves short.

6. *Volunteering:* They are actively involved in religious or charitable work and put their faith into action on a regular basis.

7. *Less prejudiced:* Their solid faith enables them to judge others' character, not their skin color, creed, or gender.

8. *Forgiving:* They are able to forgive others. Their faith enables them to let go of old hurts and get on with life.

9. *Politically involved:* They are likely to take an active interest in civic affairs.

Although I found this list to be helpful and intriguing, I think a simpler indicator of the work of the Holy Spirit in one's life, and an indicator of spiritual maturity, is found in Galatians 5:22–23—the fruit of the Spirit. Consider the degree to which you and your mate or your potential mate evidence the following traits:

- love
- joy
- peace
- patience
- kindness

- goodness
- faithfulness
- gentleness
- self-control

These are the true markers of the mature spiritual life. You can be politically involved and be active in volunteering your time, but if you are not kind to others, if your life is not filled with joy, where is the work of the Spirit? If you lack prejudice in your life, that is good, but if you are dominating and discounting with others, if you are not gentle with those in your life, where is the Spirit? If you blame and attack others for your problems, where is the peace-producing work of the Spirit?

Committed relationships, free from "come close, get away," are built on emotional and spiritual maturity. You need inner strength and fortitude to bring your full self to a relationship. These are qualities to look for in a man when considering someone who can be committed to you.

Final Thoughts

I didn't see Caroline again after her evaluation, but I've often wondered if she took my advice to carefully consider her choices in men. She had some tools for critically considering the next man who would be her mate. She seemed to understand that the patterns she had previously used were not working for her. I was confident that she would regain her children, but I was less assured that she would follow through and ask difficult questions of the men she chose to date. Asking those questions in the beginning can ease a lot of heartache down the road for Caroline or for you. Looking deep into a man's maturity during the initial stages will yield dividends later. If you are willing to be perceptive now, you will avoid relationships bound for failure.

As we consider this most difficult issue of commitment, we must ask ourselves another tough question. Have we done our own work—that is, have we worked on ourselves, on our own issues, so that we can grow up? Have we allowed the Lord to work on us to bring us to spiritual maturity? Are we entering our relationships as whole and healthy people?

If you have been intent on developing spiritual and emotional maturity, you probably have the goods necessary for a healthy, committed relationship that is free from the destructive dance of unhealthy alliances. If you have risked being close and have a history of committed relationships, a committed relationship will probably find you again. But if you possess neither the necessary skills nor the willingness to risk intimacy, a committed, emotionally vulnerable relationship will probably elude you.

I close this chapter with the words of theologian Henri Nouwen, author of *The Inner Voice of Love*. Of emotional and spiritual maturity and their impact on relationships, he writes this:

> Do not hesitate to love and love deeply. You might be afraid of the pain that deep love can cause. When those you loved deeply reject you, leave you or die, your heart will be broken. The pain that comes from deep love makes your love even more fruitful.
>
> The more you have loved and have allowed yourself to suffer because of your love, the more you will be able to let your heart grow wider and deeper. When your love is truly giving and receiving, those whom you love will not leave your heart even when they depart you. They will become part of your self and thus gradually build a community within you. Those you have deeply loved become part of you.[3]

FOUR

SABOTAGING RELATIONSHIPS

——⦿——

No one truly wishes to be unhappy, and since a lack of commitment is always the decision to be unhappy, it is clear that most couples are profoundly confused as to where their interests lie.

HUGH PRATHER

Take a right as soon as you leave the parking lot. Then another quick right and go straight. You'll see the hotel off to the right. Can't miss it. Down the road a quarter mile."

The attendant pointed out of the building and to the right.

The directions sounded easy enough, and since I had been to this hotel in Tampa previously, I was certain I would be fine. But things looked a little different in the darkness of late evening.

Fifteen minutes later, I am ashamed to say, I was exhausted, irritated, and disoriented. I did not want to admit to being lost.

Perhaps it was male pride—you know, the asking directions thing. The attendant had given clear, simple instructions. I had been to this hotel at least twice before, and yet the vaguely familiar landmarks yielded no hotel in sight. I did the only rational thing a man could do—backtrack and try again—with the exact same results.

Deeply annoyed at the attendant (simple directions, for him, were not effective for me!), I traveled further in the wrong direction, hoping to see the bright neon sign that marked my haven. No such luck.

I turned around and tried yet again. The directions had to be right, and I must have simply overlooked the hotel sign. The scenery started to look familiar, a few other hotels popping into view, but only because I had just searched this stretch of ground so many times. Alas, more of the same actions only yielded more of the same results—being lost, angry, and tired.

Finally, an hour later, in desperation I called the hotel. As I begged the clerk for directions that would guide me home, I could not conceal my frustration. I could have called half an hour earlier. I could have pulled over and asked for help. But no, pride and stubborn determination had stopped me.

"Oh no," the concerned clerk said in a barely understandable accent when I described where I was. "You going wrong direction. Turn around, follow my directions. I get you here."

I muttered something sadly close to profanity, apologized, and then issued an obligatory, faint note of gratitude for getting me back on track. Soon I would be at the hotel and in my room, albeit more than an hour later than necessary.

There I was, like so many others, going around in circles, getting nowhere fast. Rather than seeking intervention from my self-sabotage, I chose to suffer in my discomfort even though I sensed all the while that I might be lost. I had acted like this before but didn't learn from past behavior.

Women like Caroline, whom we met in the last chapter, live from event to event, crisis to crisis, traveling the same road with inappropriate directions, hoping to magically arrive at their desired destination. Not learning from past mistakes, Caroline is a living example of those who do the same thing but expect different results.

She does not see that she will not find her way because she sabotages her efforts—always ending up in situations she did not plan with men who treat her poorly, trying to navigate financial straits she had vowed never to be in. Her spirits understandably plummet. But the one constant is that she can find no rational reason why things turn out the way they do. Although she hopes for change, dreaming that her white knight will one day appear, she fails to consider the imperative of change.

Caroline lives in a state of urgency, guided from the outside in rather than from the inside out. She is paralyzed by fear—fear that she can't solve everyday problems and fear that the white knight will never ride into her life, sweep her off her feet, and commit his undying love to her. Little true change occurs, and for that reason, she can expect more of the same sabotaged behavior, more of the same troubled relationships in the future. She never stops and looks critically inward, acknowledging the necessity of change.

We hope our lives are not as chaotic as Caroline's, that they are not spun together with tangled thread. Certainly, we say, we have more clarity of purpose, more reflective activity, leading us to the glory land of determined goals that will bring meaning to our lives. We are confident, or at least hopeful, that we know how to create and sustain relationships—if only "those men" would cooperate.

Time to Reflect

Many years ago I read a book titled *The Tyranny of the Urgent*. That book had a profound impact on me, and apparently no impact at all. The fact that I can still remember its title and contents should say something. The fact that I continue to ponder its contents should also say something. But the fact that it has only negligibly altered my life is a sad commentary on my character.

The book said we tend to fill our lives with the most pressing activities. Our immediate, unfulfilled drives and needs clamor for attention. Those that are most pressing garner our attention in spite of our loftier goals. We must pay the bills, put gas in the car, do the laundry, and ferry the kids to soccer practice. Add to this most basic batch of activities other fundamentals such as making breakfast, lunch, and dinner, cleaning the house, and keeping doctor's appointments. Squeeze in an evening television program, and the day is spent—with no time for reflection or contemplation.

Add to these pressures the pleasure principle, which proposes that we seek the easiest, most satisfying path in life. Regardless of the long-term cost, too often we reach for the quickest relief from interpersonal loneliness, sadness, or other forms of pain. Rather than take the surer course toward healing, we want instant relief. We accept some cheap facsimile for love rather than seeking the real thing, and we end up sabotaging our better efforts.

I have long been an addict of both busyness and business. I seem to have an insatiable appetite for filling up every nook and cranny of my life. Although I often say that I want downtime and thoroughly enjoy quiet reflection and prayer, I do not make enough room for those things in my life. I champion those who take sabbaticals and retreat into mountain cabins alone to write and reflect, but I rarely create those opportunities for myself. And while I admire those who save up money, quit their jobs, and sail around the world or pour their hearts into missionary efforts, the thought of doing the same terrifies me. No, despite having read *The Tyranny of the Urgent*, I stick to my too-seldom-considered life.

And so the goals I set for myself, the dreams I ponder, the nudges I receive from the Holy Spirit are too often silenced by the pressing needs of the day. I feel like the apostle Paul, who said, "I can't believe myself. All of the things I would like to do, I don't end up doing. All of my wonderful plans I set for myself end up sitting on the shelf. And all the things I tell myself I will no longer do—well, I end up doing them. I sabotage myself in so many ways, and I hate it!" (Romans 7:15 paraphrased).

In an effort to combat this reluctance to embrace healthy change, I recently formed a group that reflects on the movement of God in our lives and considers creative endeavors. We are hopeful that our efforts will provide encouragement and accountability.

In Julia Cameron's *The Artist's Way*, she fervently challenges us to spend the first part of every day writing in our journals. She suggests we will meet ourselves and God on the written page and perhaps, if all goes well, align our lives with our truest calling. We will, in a perfect world, meet our shadow side and eliminate self-sabotage from our lives.

The Morning Pages, as Cameron calls them, become the meeting place for our thoughts, hopes, and dreams. In these sacred moments we will find inspirations—God-breathings. We will transcend dirty diapers, runny noses, late bills, car repairs, and misshapen love lives. We will discover or recover lost parts of ourselves, hopefully relinquishing self-sabotaging behaviors.

You might think that keeping an appointment with one's self and the Morning Pages for half an hour every day would be no big deal. Surely, scheduled time with myself and my God would surpass other more trivial matters. But if you have tried to create a similar space for daily devotions, you know that the Saboteur will also greet you at the door of your prayer and journaling room. Who was it that said, "The road to hell is paved with good intentions"?

When we devalue self-reflection and God-reflection, we sabotage our time for God and for planning important personal changes. Caroline, you, and I all need to make sure we set aside time to reflect on the direction of our lives.

One Woman's Self-Sabotage

Gail is a 50-something divorced woman with enhanced blonde hair and a bold, stylish presence. A large and flamboyant woman, this perfectly dressed banker came to see me in an attempt to understand and eliminate her self-defeating patterns.

"What brings you to counseling?" I asked during our first session.

With a gravelly voice that hinted at a chronic smoking habit, she said, "I can't seem to attract anything but 'players,' and I'm sick of it. Sometimes I just feel like giving up. I don't know why I am a sucker for those kinds of men, but I am. I want to learn why I keep making the same mistakes."

"What exactly is a player?" I asked naïvely.

"You know. Guys who are just out to have fun. They like 'arm-candy' but don't want anything serious."

"You're attracted to these kinds of men, and they are attracted to you?"

"I guess so," she said smiling.

"You undoubtedly have some powerful attractions to these kinds of men."

"They're fun. They're exciting. And they seem attracted to me—at least at first. But things always end up going sour."

"What does that mean?"

"Well, like I said, they're fun for a while, but I want something permanent, and they want to move on. The party scene is a whole lot less attractive to me now than it was several years ago."

"Leaving you wondering what happened?"

"Yes. But they're so much fun at the time," she said.

"Why do you smile when you say that?" I asked.

"I guess because I feel embarrassed. I know that I can attract these men. Don't get me wrong—there are things about it that I enjoy. But I know better. I should know what I'm doing, but I keep making mistakes. Something I am doing must tell men I am available for short-term relationships—and I'm not!"

"Mistakes are easy to make, especially if we don't know why or even how we are making them. Have you given much thought to your dating patterns?"

"No, I suppose not. I just keep falling into these bad situations. I am forever picking up the pieces of my romantic life. I can handle my accounts at the bank easily enough, but I can't seem to handle men. I'm not sure I can figure out what makes you guys tick," she added.

"Well, if it makes you feel any better, I think men are equally confused when it comes to women."

I asked Gail to tell me more about her history. She had recently ended a one-year relationship with a real estate developer. She had hoped the relationship would end at the altar. Instead, it ended with him telling her, in no uncertain terms, that he was never going to get married again and that he hoped she would understand.

"Why would I understand that?" Gail said sarcastically. "Like he thinks I'm going to throw my morals out the window and move in with him for the next 30 years. I'll admit I've been a fool in the past and compromised my values, but I'm not that big a fool now."

"Did his announcement take you by surprise?"

"Well, yes and no. He had hinted at his position before, but I guess I didn't want to hear it. I have been hinting at marriage for months, and he got squeamish every time I brought it up. Deep in my heart I knew it wasn't going to work. I just hoped that somehow I could change his mind. Crazy, huh?"

"No, not crazy at all. We all do things that we know are not in our best interest. We pay attention to one part of the picture and ignore the part that creates anxiety for us. But it's good news that you're here to look more closely at your patterns."

Gail took a deep breath and sighed loudly.

"You're tired of these patterns, aren't you?" I said.

She began to cry.

"I'm just tired of being alone. My divorce four years ago hurt really bad. Every time I think I've found someone to share my life with, things fall apart. I'm angry with myself and with the men who treat me this way. I just want it to stop."

"The good news is this—anything that we can predict, we can prevent. If we can understand the patterns and see how we keep repeating them, we stand a good chance of changing them. Now, let's look more closely at both your history and your more recent patterns."

I worked with Gail for several months. She made great progress. She came to understand how hurt she had been when her 25-year marriage ended and how lonely and incomplete she felt afterward. She wanted desperately to fill the void, and she discovered that the attention she received for her attractive and provocative appearance from "players" helped ease her pain.

At first Gail downplayed this aspect of her character. However, she slowly began to see that she liked being with men who were charismatic and who lavished attention, fancy nightlife, and gifts on her. She had never really understood that these qualities she enjoyed were shallow and could easily be self-defeating. She hadn't seen that she was trying to treat an inner wound with attention from men or that the men who would lavish this attention on her were often least likely to be interested in a lasting commitment.

Gail had healing work to do. Not only did she have to withdraw from the lure of the players' attention, she also had to deal with rejection wounds from her divorce that gave rise to her excessive desire for their attention. She also needed to realize that a man with emotional and spiritual integrity may not be as suave and charismatic as some of the men she was used to dating. It was not an easy adjustment but a necessary one.

Players and Partners

Are you one of those women who rail against players—men who are perfectly willing to use you for their own selfish desires with little regard for your well-being? Many women like Gail are angry at these men. Ironically, these women fail to stop and think that players must have partners in order to continue their escapades. Without partners, there would be no players.

Players are almost always engaged in serial dating. They are playing the field, with little desire for a long-term, committed relationship. Involving yourself with one of these men will only lead to trouble and pain for you.

John Gray, author of the bestseller *Men are from Mars, Women are from Venus,* wrote an article about self-sabotaging relationships in the world of dating titled "Are You Sabotaging Your Chances of Finding Love?" He says that women frequently do things that damage their ability to find love and suggests the following five questions to consider in your quest for love.

1. *Are you serially dating?* Gray says many people constantly date someone new. They believe they can always find a bigger, better deal. "For them, the grass is always greener on the other side of the fence. What they find out later is that the water bill is higher, too. Serial daters are people who are open to dating someone until the big 'C' is mentioned (that would be commitment), and then they miraculously find someone more attractive, more their type, more into the things that they would like to do for fun." He adds that if you are going through a stage where you want to be dating for fun, serial dating is not a problem. However, if you desire a long-term relationship, serial dating is probably a self-sabotaging behavior.

2. *Do you take emotional risks?* Gray stresses the importance of being open and vulnerable with the person you are dating and expecting that in return. Being open and honest can be frightening, but it is a sign of a deeper level of commitment. When the moment presents itself, do you and your partner risk emotional vulnerability or the safer path of self-protection? Does your man let you do all the talking? If so, this is a sign and should alert you to the possibility of both a lack of commitment and self-sabotage.

3. *When the option is doing something new or doing the same thing you have done before, which do you choose?* Gray suggests that you may need to be open to changing for the sake of your love relationship rather than settling into your well-worn routine. "Sometimes the very reason we are alone is that we are unwilling to step outside of our comfort zone and try something new. This can be as simple as trying a new type of food or seeing a new type of movie. Or it can be bigger things like learning to have more fun and take life less seriously." When the opportunity arises, do you allow yourself to try something new and different?

4. *How well do you listen to your partner?* Being a good listener in your relationships is very important. Instead of giving what you would like to receive in your relationship, listen to your partner to determine what he truly wants. Gray suggests that you try an experiment. Engage in a conversation with a stranger, asking how he feels about a certain issue. Listen deeply to what he is saying. What is the meaning behind his words? Are you able to articulate it? Obviously, this skill is a critical aspect of relating. If you have not cultivated it, you may be hampering your relationships.

5. *How do you want to continue, now that you are aware of your actions?* Gray emphasizes that with new understanding about yourself you are prepared to change. "If you are doing things that unknowingly sabotage your relationships, what do you want to do differently now that you know this? Nothing bad can come of trying something new...After all, they say the definition of insanity is doing the same thing over and over again, hoping for different results."[1]

Choosing the Wrong Man Over and Over

So many women choose the wrong man over and over again. While on the surface this may seem easy to remedy, it is not necessarily so. This is because we are creatures of habits, patterns, and ritualized behavior. We find a familiar way of relating and then cling to it for dear life.

I receive several e-mails each week from people who have read one of my books. A woman recently wrote this:

"Dear Dr. Hawkins, I have a pattern of choosing the wrong men over and over again. After being attracted to them I find out they are either married, already in a relationship, or are workaholics or alcoholics. Most of the time they lead me on, and then I find out the rest of the story about them. What am I doing wrong?"

Although I have no simple answer for this woman, clearly she is exhibiting self-sabotaging behavior. She notes that she repeatedly chooses the wrong men. She shares how she moves forward before finding out "the rest of the story." This tells us she has some unconscious pattern of behavior that, fortunately, she can overcome with counseling. Why does she move ahead without having all the facts? What might her core problems be?

Low self-esteem: This woman quite likely has low self-esteem and finds men who know this and take advantage of it. She likely feels that she is not good enough to attract someone who is truly available and thus more difficult to attract. Because she may feel that she does not measure up, seeking someone who could really care about her would be threatening. Tragically, her behavior only reinforces her low self-esteem—rejection upon rejection adds insult to her injury.

Fear of being alone: Many women choose unavailable men because they are afraid of being alone. Being with someone, even if only for a short season, is better than taking the time necessary to find a quality man. These women believe a temporary fix is better than a long-term solution. However, this is a sure way to sabotage efforts for long-term happiness.

Fear of closeness: Just like men who will not let themselves get too close to a woman, women who play out destructive, self-sabotaging behaviors again and again usually have their own fears of closeness. They choose players for the immediate thrill and attention they receive, but like the players themselves, they are unwilling to commit to a relationship for the long haul.

Fear of commitment: Yes, women have fears of commitment just as men do. They are often reluctant to label those fears, but they are there. These women say that they want to be close but then avoid men who might encourage commitment.

Fear of change: Most of us are addicts of familiarity. We may espouse change, but we resist it. We rant and rave about our conditions, yet we do little to really change them. Perhaps this is a pattern for you. You say that you want a man who is available, but you invariably find such men inadequate in some way. Or perhaps you find yourself seeking the same kind of man over and over again because you find safety in the familiar.

I remember working with a 60-year-old woman named Betty who married alcoholic men. Modestly attractive, she took great pride in her meticulously coiffed white hair and expensive jewelry. Betty came to see me because she was deeply in love with a man who she feared was "just like my two previous husbands, who were alcoholics." Listen to Betty's story.

"I can't seem to help myself. I have been married twice before to professional men who work 65 hours a week. They come home after they have had too much to drink, drink their way through dinner, and pass out in front of the television. I keep thinking I am through with them, and then I meet another one. Nothing seems to change."

As I explored Betty's history, I discovered that she had spent many lonely years mired in these relationships with her alcoholic husbands. She had never worked outside the home and was dependent on her husbands to keep her living in the grand style she had become accustomed to. Beneath her facade was an empty, fearful woman.

"I have always felt insecure," she told me. "These men never made me feel good. They were married to their booze, not to me. But they told me they loved me, and I always settled for that. I'm tired of living like this."

"So you're ready to make a change?"

"Well, you would certainly think so. But I seem to be falling into the same old pattern with my current boyfriend, Jack. He is just like the others. I can't stand my current situation, but I also can't stand the thought of leaving. The thought of being alone again frightens me."

Consistent with her previous behavior, Betty was in a relationship with an alcoholic. She used many different thinking errors to justify staying in the relationship. She claimed to be surprised to find out how much he drank. She also insisted she was surprised to find out that he was not willing to commit to marriage or even exclusive dating. In fact, he had the audacity to expect her to be intimate with him while he continued dating other women. She sabotaged herself at every turn.

Her friends wondered why Betty was surprised. The evidence was right in front of her face, but she could never see it. The answer lies in Betty's low self-esteem and fear of being alone, along with her desperate desire to make the relationship work.

Desperation and unconscious self-defeating behaviors create powerful repetitive patterns in our lives. Only as Betty became willing to carefully examine those patterns and change them was she able to avoid alcoholics and seek healthier men.

Dangerous Men

One of the surest ways to sabotage your relationship is to link up with a dangerous and therefore unavailable man. Alcoholism is only one of many reasons some men are dangerous. Remember that for a man to be emotionally or physically available, he must be emotionally healthy. Dangerous men are anything but healthy.

- They have one or more chronic unhealthy behavior patterns.
- They refuse to treat you with respect.
- They cannot commit to a relationship.
- They may have a significant personality disorder, such as antisocial personality patterns.
- They have a weak and shallow spiritual life.
- They are verbally abusive and manipulative.
- They are unable to truly listen to you and champion you.
- They appear willing to commit but then back away when faced with an opportunity to follow through.

Perhaps you find yourself choosing men who are dangerous—all the while insisting that they'll change. You tell yourself lies in order to convince yourself that they really aren't all that dangerous. Many women I have worked with use multiple "thinking errors" to convince themselves that things are not as bad as they appear. See if you recognize yourself in any of these self-defeating patterns of thinking:

- "He's really not that bad. After all, he loves me."

- "He really isn't drinking that much. And he says he can quit anytime."
- "He only treats me badly when he's stressed out."
- "He learned that behavior from his parents."
- "All men are like that."
- "I know that he has problems, but I can help him through them."
- "He's not abusive. He just has a temper problem when stressed-out."
- "At least he comes home to me every night."
- "I know he'll change in the future."

A close look at the list above reveals the thinking errors that perpetuate dysfunctional behavior. Look closely and you will see errors such as minimizing problems, justifying wrong and dangerous behaviors, wishful, naïve thinking, and even the *messiah complex*—"I know I can fix him." Each erroneous thinking style leads to only one end—being stuck in a relationship with a man who is unable to commit physically, emotionally, or both.

You may find the above list a bit daunting. Are there any men who could actually pass the "dangerous man" test? Yes, of course there are.

Then where are they? We will address that later in this book.

Givers, Takers, and Sharers

Another reason people sometimes settle for less is that they see people only as givers or takers.

In an article titled "Is Not Knowing and Using This Simple Concept Sabotaging Your Relationships and Destroying Your Happiness?" Bryan Redfield writes, "One of the biggest traps I've seen people who are unsuccessful in relationships fall into is they believe there are only two kinds of people: Givers and Takers. As a result they end up being used."

Redfield goes on to say that takers are selfish while givers are unselfish. This is a great arrangement—for the taker. But for the giver, it can be very abusive. Eventually, after years of pain, givers often succumb to depression, anxiety, and chronic low self-esteem. Takers end up being self-centered, arrogant egoists.

Christians tend to be especially confused about this issue of giving and taking, a topic I wrote about extensively in my book *When Pleasing Others Is Hurting You*. Too often, Christians are uncertain whether they should demand respect in a relationship. Because of Scriptures that exhort us that "It is more blessed to give than to receive" (Acts 20:35), we ignore other Scriptures that exhort us to love ourselves *as* we love others. Subsequently, life becomes unbalanced.

Redfield admits that he used to be a giver—one who gave and gave beyond the point of reason. He gave well beyond what would be considered appropriate, using Scriptures such as Galatians 6, which encourages us to "bear one another's burdens." He assisted others when he could have been more helpful by letting them assist themselves. He gave and gave out of false humility. The result was disastrous. People took advantage of his generosity, leaving him feeling resentful and bitter.

Redfield was frustrated with the patterns he repeated and the negative impact they were having on his relationships. He explains that he asked a friend how she was able to command a man's respect *and keep it*. "I could learn something that would help me out of my emotionally abused rut to use with the next woman I got involved with." Her response is worth considering.

> Bryan, it's really simple. Everyone in abusive relationships thinks there are only two groups of people: Givers and Takers. But there's a third group. And once you understand that, it all starts to fall into place and your relationships start to work out. The third group is Sharers. Sharers know in their mind, heart, and soul that they deserve to receive as well as give. Sharers

know that healthy relationships balance out to be 50/50 give and take. Sharers have a healthy self-respect, and they expect their partner to treat them with respect, the same respect they give their partner.[2]

The advice from Redfield's friend may have been inspired by the Scriptures. Certainly the Scriptures encourage us to be givers, but not in a self-destructive way that enables other people's abusive behavior. We are told to mutually give, to "submit to one another out of reverence for Christ" (Ephesians 5:21).

Christ shares a parable that illustrates the importance of being responsible in your giving to others. In Matthew 25, Jesus tells the story of ten virgins who took their lamps out to meet a bridegroom. Five were foolish and five were wise. Five were prepared for the momentous occasion; five were not. The foolish ones took their lamps out to meet the bridegroom but did not take any oil with them. The other five were responsible and took oil with them. When the call went out that the bridegroom was near, hours after they had all fallen asleep, the wise ones were able to trim their lamps and greet him appropriately. The foolish ones asked for oil from the others but were told there was not enough. So the foolish ones rushed off to obtain oil, but they were too late to attend the wedding banquet.

This is an interesting parable. Many of us would have given our oil to the others who were asking for it. Turning someone away in their time of need would have been difficult. Yet we see in this story that the needy ones set themselves up for their plight—they failed to prepare. Giving in to their request would have simply enabled their irresponsible behavior—they would have learned nothing, repeating their self-sabotaging behavior again in the future.

We are admonished repeatedly in Scripture to be wise and responsible, caring for ourselves and others appropriately. Even Jesus, the Author of love and sacrificial giving, allows for consequences of irresponsible behavior.

Changing Self-Sabotaging Behavior

You have undoubtedly picked up this book because you are tired of being in a relationship that lacks committed intimacy. You want a man who is not only physically available but emotionally available as well. Having what you want is possible, but first you must understand what you are doing that is preventing this from happening. That probably includes some self-defeating behaviors.

Having read this chapter, you may now be familiar with some of your patterns—and that is a critical first step. Understanding self-sabotaging patterns and taking ownership of them is a powerful beginning to healing. Self-sabotaging behavior often occurs because we are unaware of our destructive tendencies and hidden motives. And fear is typically the culprit. Fortunately, facing our fears creates opportunities to change and heal from these destructive patterns.

Perhaps you could see yourself in Gail's story. She discovered that she had self-esteem problems that only worsened when she chose men who made her feel important temporarily but created a negative vicious circle in the long run. She had never interrupted her cycle before, but now, through counseling, prayer, and Bible study, she was able to make significant strides in improving her self-esteem.

Gail had to practice new, challenging beliefs as well as new behaviors in order for real healing to occur. In addition to admitting her self-destructive tendency to seek men who would cater to her attractiveness, making her feel worthwhile and "complete" for the moment, she had to practice other skills. She practiced meditating on Scriptures that affirmed her worth as a child of God. She found special strength in Psalm 103:2-5:

> Praise the LORD, O my soul,
>   and forget not all his benefits—
> who forgives all your sins
>   and heals all your diseases,

who redeems your life from the pit
  and crowns you with love and compassion,
who satisfies your desires with good things
  so that your youth is renewed like the eagle's.

Gail also joined a women's support group at her church where she acknowledged her difficulties. She found this support critical to her growth. Sharing her vulnerabilities and being affirmed by other women were decisive steps in her progress. There she talked about her choices, received affirmation for her ability to choose wisely, and accepted accountability for her decisions.

Perhaps most important to Gail was her decision to love herself enough to insist on dating only men who were healthy and who would affirm her in positive ways. She has learned how to determine if a man is dangerous, and this has made a great deal of difference. She is a child of God, as are you, and worthy of being loved completely. Her new verse of affirmation and direction is Colossians 1:10-12. This verse can be a powerful help to you as well.

And we pray this in order that you may live a life worthy of the Lord and may please him in every way: bearing fruit in every good work, growing in the knowledge of God, being strengthened with all power according to his glorious might so that you may have great endurance and patience, and joyfully giving thanks to the Father, who has qualified you to share in the inheritance of the saints in the kingdom of light.

FIVE

Not Ready for Prime Time

*Be patient toward all that is unfinished in your heart and
try to love the questions themselves...Do not now seek the
answers which cannot be given you because you would not
be able to live them and the point is to live everything.*

RAINIER MARIA RILKE, *Letters to a Young Poet*

Nineteen-seventy-six. The Vietnam War was officially over,
the world was relatively peaceful once again, and I was finished with school. After six consecutive years of higher education,
I was excited about entering the field of counseling. I was also
ready to throw my books off the nearest bridge and scream aloud
that I was a free man. I was more than ready to finally be able to
spend an entire weekend in mindless play.

Quite surprisingly I was sidetracked from my career goals
by an opportunity to sing and play trumpet in a contemporary

Christian band—an inauspicious group called The Sounds of Isaac. The band was a ragtag group with a modicum of talent that simply enjoyed the chance to sing and play. I agreed to join them, and our group quickly became my part-time passion.

As the months went by, our band became quite good. Requests for our performances crept in at first and then arrived with more frequency. George, a high school math teacher by day and our manager by night, encouraged and organized us. He booked our gigs, which ranged from ice cream parlors, schools, and churches to a performance at a Luis Palau gathering in Portland, Oregon. The possibilities appeared limitless as we practiced harder and gradually set our sights higher.

George was a husky man with a wry sense of humor. He bought all the latest sound and recording equipment and teased the group with the possibility of going big time, which meant that we would tour and might get picked up by a recording company. Although we initially dissed his vision of notoriety, we secretly wondered if he might be onto something.

We practiced a lot—up to two nights a week. My part-time passion became an obsession. This venture assumed control of my thoughts and dreams. Would we, could we, go further? One day this question came to a head. Wade, our lead vocalist, a strikingly good-looking and charismatic young man, asked for a special meeting of the band. He announced that he was ready to take the group to the next level. It would require more hours of practice, more investment of money for advertising and equipment, more commitment of energy, more travel. I distinctly remember my reaction. Not "I wonder what this might be like," but an emphatic "No!"

Wade insisted that this move was the logical next step, but it didn't feel right to me. He was ready to put other aspects of his life on hold to pursue this dream, but I was not. I simply was not prepared to commit myself to such a rigorous schedule of travel.

I was not ready to make the sacrifices necessary to support such a decision.

When several of us declined Wade's offer, the band parted ways. Wade took his skills to the next level, working as a professional singer. He was willing to make the sacrifices and devote the necessary energy to become a professional. I was not.

It wasn't that I was afraid of such a move—I was simply not ready for it. I was not prepared to make the commitment Wade was demanding.

The Importance of Timing

Just as I was not ready to commit myself fully to the band, so your man may not be ready to commit himself to a long-term relationship. Several stages are involved in building a relationship and attaining commitment. I call the first stage "not ready for prime time."

My friend Kevin believes in the proper timing of things. He conducts his life on the premise that things work out the way they are supposed to. Sometimes his inklings have a spiritual bent to them—other times he calls them hunches.

I once asked Kevin, a shrewd and talented businessman, to consider joining me in a coffee shop enterprise, something near and dear to my heart. For me, a daily latté or two is a prerequisite to normal, healthy functioning. I need my daily fix of the frothy milk-caffeine-foam-coffee mixture. Folgers stopped cutting it years ago.

I presented my case to Kevin: We should join forces and open either an espresso stand or a coffee shop. He was mildly interested but lacked the zeal I had hoped for. He offered a perfunctory willingness to talk about a business enterprise, but enthusiasm was missing. After a number of hours of discussing possible places and opportunities, he finally got around to having The Talk with me.

"David," he said. "I just don't feel right about this project. I think the coffee thing is a good idea, and I think there is money to be made in it, but I don't feel right about it. I'm not sure why I'm not ready to commit myself to it. But I need to follow my intuition."

Obviously, this was not what I wanted to hear. Kevin had money, brains, business acumen, and vision. He could read the entrepreneurial climate and make things happen. But my timing was off. He just was not ready for this commitment.

I tried unsuccessfully to talk him out of his position. No luck. I tried to pin him down about his reluctance. Still no luck. He was simply not ready to make the move, and that was that. Deal over. We scuttled the mission, and I moved my coffee dreams to the back burner.

Thankfully, that was not the end of the coffee shop saga. Even as I write these words, years after my encounter with Kevin, I have met three friends, Bill, Liz, and Christie, who are excited about starting a coffee business.

In a story that would take too long to tell, Bill, Christie, and I crossed paths and struck up a friendship. Months later, in a most unusual encounter in a coffee shop far off the beaten trail in a small town near Hoodsport, Washington, Bill, Christie, Liz (the coffee shop owner), and I began conversing about opening a business of our own.

That conversation evolved into more serious discussions, and at this time we are considering joining forces in a coffee shop venture. The timing seems right, the players are ready, and prime time may not be far away. Years of dreaming and preparation—along with a healthy dose of God's timing—may be coming together in an exciting way.

In a few months, I may be wearing a T-shirt with a cute logo of a man drinking a latté.

A Time for Everything

Certainly there is a right timing for everything. The wisdom writer, Solomon, noted this:

> There is a time for everything, and a season for every activity under heaven…He has made everything beautiful in its time. He has also set eternity in the hearts of men; yet they cannot fathom what God has done from beginning to end (Ecclesiastes 3:1,11).

Could he really mean a time for *everything?*

This passage is profound in its simplicity. Listen again to the words that assure us that there is indeed a season for *everything*—including relationships.

> A time to be born and a time to die,
> a time to plant and a time to uproot,
> a time to kill and a time to heal,
> a time to tear down and a time to build,
> a time to weep and a time to laugh,
> a time to mourn and a time to dance,
> a time to scatter stones and a time to gather them,
> a time to embrace and a time to refrain,
> a time to search and a time to give up,
> a time to keep and a time to throw away,
> a time to tear and a time to mend,
> a time to be silent and a time to speak,
> a time to love and a time to hate,
> a time for war and a time for peace (Ecclesiastes 3:2-8).

Recently I heard a friend of mine explain that she is trying to live more honestly with this passage. Sharon is working hard to be a better steward of her personal and professional time. Rather than hanging on tenaciously to some endeavor long past its expiration date, she does her best to be sensitive to God's timing. She now has a better understanding of when it is time to plant and time to uproot, when it is time to tear down and time to build up. She considers the passage an invaluable piece of wisdom in her decision making.

Sharon told me she had been struggling with letting a women's group dissolve because of lack of interest. Although she loves this support group, which has met many important needs over the past several years, she senses that its time may be coming to an end. She might be able to use her energies more effectively in some other way.

God's providential timing is not always easy for me to live with because I want to do things in my own time. When I desire something, I want it right then. I do not want to wait for it to arrive at its own pace.

God often uses circumstances to demonstrate the proper timing of things, but carefully assessing those circumstances is extremely difficult for me. Most of us have an insatiable penchant for pressing forward in spite of cautionary signs to the contrary. We must temper that desire.

When a Man Isn't Ready

Every relationship has a time when people are simply not ready to commit. This does not mean they are afraid to commit or are commitment-phobic. It also doesn't mean that they are dysfunctional or have long-standing character issues. It simply means they are not yet ready to commit.

This man who is not yet ready must be distinguished from the one who never will be ready to commit. There is a world of difference—and the distinction is critical.

Simon, later called Peter, is a perfect example of a man who was not yet ready for prime time. You recall that when Jesus chose Peter to be a disciple, He changed his name. But this outer change, a superficial alteration suggesting powerful movement in the future, was not enough to render an inner transformation and full commitment to Christ. Peter needed far more life experience to prepare for ultimate commitment.

Impetuous, impatient Peter followed Christ with zeal, to be sure. He seemed to be in the thick of each of Jesus' powerful encounters. You cannot help but admire his enthusiasm. He let his lips lead the way and gave thoughtful consideration later. In spite of his powerful name, Peter—The Rock—still was not yet ready for a committed life of obedience to Christ.

The ultimate test came when Christ prepared for His ascension. When He shared with His disciples that He would be leaving, Peter insisted that he was ready for the ultimate sacrifice, the ultimate commitment. He said, "I will lay down my life for you" (John 13:37).

Jesus rebuked him. "Peter," He said (paraphrased), "You say you will lay down your life for me, but you won't even stand up for me. You will deny you even knew me when the going gets tough." Ouch! And Peter thought he was ready for prime time. (We know that Peter later made it to prime time—his leadership was foundational in the emerging church.)

Letting Things Unfold Naturally

Kathleen and Rick came to see me for counseling. They were both 30 years old and had been dating for nearly a year. Kathleen was a soft-spoken and elegant interior designer with a thriving private practice in a small community not far from my office. Rick was a tall, muscular, hard-working electrical contractor from the same area. They had met on a job site and began dating soon after.

Their relationship developed swiftly. They spent a great deal of time together, shared spiritual and moral values, and had similar family backgrounds. They enjoyed professional sports events as well as quiet times reading books together. Kathleen had expected a ring to be forthcoming, but discussions on that front stalled. Whenever the topic of commitment and marriage came up, Rick balked. He wanted more time. Kathleen then pushed for counseling, and Rick reluctantly agreed.

"So, tell me some more about your relationship and what has brought you to counseling," I said at our first meeting.

Rick looked at Kathleen, nodding for her to start.

"Okay," she said to him. "I can share things from my point of view. But I want to hear from you too."

"Not a problem," he said.

They sat close to one another on the small sofa in my office. She reached for his hand, which he offered quickly.

"I think we're ready to take the next step in our relationship. We have been together nearly a year, and I think it's time to get engaged. We have shared our love for each other, and I don't know why we can't move forward. I don't know what the problem is."

Kathleen made it clear that she was ready to move to the next level in the relationship. She wanted a ring as a token of Rick's commitment to her and a promise of marriage. She felt that his reluctance was simply another indicator that he was not the right man for her.

"So what is your take on this?" I asked Rick.

"Well, that's the crazy thing. I don't think we have a problem. I love Kathleen, but I'm just not ready to take that next step yet. I know that I will be eventually, but right now I'm not. I am still willing to date her exclusively, but I am not ready for the ring. I don't understand why anything is wrong with that."

"So, Rick," I said, "are you in love with Kathleen?"

"Yes, absolutely."

"But you feel you're being pressured to make a final decision when you're not ready to do so?"

"Yes. Kathleen and I are still getting to know each other. We're still working out some important kinks in our relationship. I really enjoy her, and like I said, I love her, but I'm still sorting things through."

"Still working some things through? I don't get that," Kathleen said. "That says to me that you're not sure about us and that I might be just wasting my time."

"That's not at all what I mean. I meant exactly what I said. I'm still preparing myself for a lifetime of commitment to you. That's it."

Kathleen pulled her hand away from Rick, clearly annoyed.

"What's wrong?" I asked.

"When I hear him say that he has some things to sort out, that just gives me a bad feeling. It's like he's saying that this relationship might not be permanent."

"And that's how our fights go," Rick said. "I say what I'm thinking and then get punished for it."

"Kathleen, you hear trouble, but Rick says there isn't any."

"That's what he says, but I'd like to know what you think, Dr. Hawkins."

"It seems to me that you both just need a little more time to enjoy and appreciate your relationship," I said. "To be truthful, Kathleen, I don't hear any danger signals. I don't hear any serious problems. I just think you both need a little more time—time set aside to simply have fun with each other and eventually talk more about your future."

"You think I might be setting myself up for a big fall?" Kathleen asked.

"No, I don't. I hear that Rick is 'in' but that he needs more time. If you push him, he is likely to react and push back."

"That makes a lot of sense to me," Rick said. "You've expressed exactly what I've been trying to say all along. I'm just not ready yet. It doesn't mean that I won't be ready. I just need Kathleen to relax and enjoy our relationship. I have no intention of hurting her."

Kathleen seemed to soften. She looked at Rick and reached again for his hand.

"So, how about it, Kathleen? Is he worth giving some more time to? Is it worth it to you to take a chance and let this relationship unfold naturally?"

"Definitely," she said. "I guess I do need to relax. I have to keep things in perspective."

"That would sure help me a bunch," Rick added.

"I know that this won't be easy for me," she said. "I listen to my girlfriends, and they tell me to watch myself. But I don't think Rick would intentionally hurt me. And I do think he loves me."

Letting Him Not Be Ready

Understanding that he simply is not yet ready is one thing. To *let that be* is quite another—to let him have his time to prepare himself to commit to you, to let him have his time to get ready for a lifetime of commitment.

Mark Nepo, in his wonderful book *The Book of Awakening,* shares an account of his impatience with love. He writes, "At times in my life, I have wanted love so badly that I have reimagined myself, reinvented who I am, in an attempt to be more desirable and more deserving, only to discover again and again, that it is the tending of my own soul that invites the natural processes of love to begin."[1]

Nepo speaks a language we can all understand. Being patient and letting love take its course can be painfully difficult. I want to emphasize that giving someone time is not an indication of being foolish in love and commitment, but rather a sign of being patient when we know a situation is right.

Something, perhaps a deep-rooted fear, makes you want to push things. You want to make something happen, not trusting that he, and God, will treat you fairly. You want to micromanage things to improve your chances of securing a committed relationship. But that is not how it works. If you fence him in, he will recoil. It is a man's natural and very primitive response to being cornered.

And so, for the meantime, your task is to let him not be ready. It's okay. He simply is *not yet* ready for prime time. In all likelihood, he will be, in time.

Redefining Singleness

Being single is not easy—especially in our culture, which places so much emphasis on being connected, married, or in a serious relationship. This adulation of being married is sometimes quite subtle and sometimes not so subtle at all.

Consider that many churches still have no singles programs. Consider that we applaud those who have stayed married for many years even though some of those marriages may be filled with violence. We feel a huge amount of pressure to be paired up.

The famed psychoanalyst Erik Erikson, in his book *Childhood and Society,* talks about the moratorium most primitive cultures observe—that time when an individual is irresponsible and dependent before settling down with a mate and having children.

Our culture does not encourage this. The closest we come to it is high school and college, where we allow people (for a very short time) to be confused about life and to be single. For that brief time, people do not need to know exactly what they are going to be in life. Still, that does not stop the endless parade of well-meaning adults from asking, "So what are you going to do after you graduate?"

Harville Hendrix, in his book *Keeping the Love You Find,* shares some interesting insights into this problem.

> We need to redefine singleness, to update the rules, and to educate singles as to the purpose and benefits of this vital transition. I suggest the best way to accomplish this is to institute a modernized version of Erikson's moratorium. In our society we hold up to young people a model of early decision and commitment as to life's path, and then we end up with burned-out executives

and displaced homemakers thirty years down the line.[2]

Hendrix goes on to say that we should not see singleness in a negative light, but in fact, we should recognize it as a vital stage of the journey to maturation.

> It is a time to learn who we are, to learn responsibility and self-sufficiency, to identify our true desires, and to confront our inner strengths and demons, a time to make changes in the things that stymie our pleasure and progress in life, to learn how to connect and communicate on all levels. It would be sorely needed relationship training.[3]

He believes that those who make this necessary journey will avoid costly errors in the long run.

Hendrix appropriately connects some of these issues to midlife singleness as well. Certainly I have found that those who have experienced a failed marriage or two face many of the same problems adolescents face. Those coming out of a failed marriage often have self-esteem questions, identity issues, and fears about their future. Too often, they believe they can resolve these problems through marriage. "Even forced, unwanted singleness can be a blessing in disguise, a time for healing and reestablishing one's priorities and sense of oneself."[4]

This in-between time can be a wonderful occasion for reconnecting with yourself and renewing your relationship with the Lord by learning to trust Him in new ways. It is a time to affirm Solomon's words: "Trust in the LORD with all your heart and lean not on your own understanding; in all your ways acknowledge him, and he will make your paths straight" (Proverbs 3:5-6).

Reconnecting with Yourself

This "not yet ready for prime time" moment provides an excellent opportunity to reconnect with yourself. Far from being a selfish and sinful thing to do, developing a legitimate self to bring to your relationship is absolutely necessary. You cannot expect your mate to make you feel whole, healthy, or stable. You must handle those issues with God.

Trauma and times of emotional upheaval can stifle or strain a healthy relationship with the self and with God. They can also easily be times of disconnection. How many divorced people leave the church, never to return? How many people going through emotional turmoil push away from any kind of intimacy, fearing that their struggles will be exposed? And yet the church and God's loving hand of healing are needed all the more during these times.

Recently, I received an e-mail from a woman who complained bitterly about her loveless marriage. She recounted years of emotional violence in her relationship and the toll it had taken on her emotionally. I expected her to state that she was ready to leave her husband and offer supporting evidence for that decision. Surprisingly, she said, "While I am unhappy in my marriage, I have found it to be a very fruitful time spiritually. Without these difficulties, I would never have the rich relationship I now enjoy with God. So I am thankful for the problems. I am not sure what will happen in my marriage, but I know God is with me and will take me through whatever I will face in the future. I trust Him to give me the courage to face my problems and to make wise decisions about the things that need to be changed."

This woman's journey is not meant to be prescriptive. But it illustrates that times of struggle may be times of disconnection for some people, while for others they are rich times of learning and even reconnecting with deeper parts of themselves. Certainly these difficult times are opportunities to develop a richer relationship with God.

Henri Nouwen, in his book *The Inner Voice of Love*, writes about the healing potential of this time between relationships. He is sympathetic to the desire to be in a relationship but also notes that this period can offer fertile growth emotionally and spiritually.

> It is not easy to stay with your loneliness. The temptation is to mask your pain or to escape into fantasies about people who will take it away. But when you can acknowledge your loneliness in a safe, contained place, you make your pain available to God's healing.[5]

Deciding When the Time Is Right

I can hear some of you shouting, "So how will I know whether he is just not ready or he is stalling for eternity?"

This is an important question. You *must* be able to know when he is serious and when he is messing with your mind. Effectively assessing this situation will reduce your chances of being hurt.

First, *the responsibility for your well-being is in your hands, not his.* You must cultivate the necessary skills so that you will know when to say when. You cannot give the responsibility for your life over to him. If you rely on your partner to take care of you, you will be hurt time and again. No one will look after you the way you can look after you.

Second, *relationships will always contain an element of risk.* No one wants to hear that. You don't want to enter into something that could backfire on you. You don't want to be left alone and heartbroken. You don't want to be left crying when he walks out the door. Being rejected is painful. But you must take the risk if you want a chance at a healthy, rewarding relationship.

Third, *you can minimize the risks by playing it smart and gathering information.* Keep your eyes and ears open.

During my sons' adolescent years they talked about a principle I'd like to pass on to you: the DTR. "What in the world is DTR?" I asked them. They looked at me as if I had just fallen off a turnip truck. "It's Determine The Relationship." I asked for an explanation.

"The DTR," Josh said impatiently, "is when you talk about where you are in the relationship and whether it has a future. Everybody has a DTR moment after they are with someone for a while." I have shared this sound advice with many of my clients.

Fourth, *process the information as accurately as possible.* Obviously, information can be invaluable, but not if we distort it to mean anything we want. Kathleen was receiving important information about Rick's commitment to her, but she was distorting it to mean that he might walk out any day. Work hard to get good information, and then check with your partner to make sure it is accurate.

Fifth, *rely on confidants who can help you process information when necessary.* Having someone close to you who will help you analyze messages and intentions is very important. When deciding on the issue of levels of commitment, you will benefit from having someone who will help you process the information. Accuracy and objectivity are critical.

Sixth, *become an expert discerner of character and integrity.* To some extent, you are placing your life in another's hands. You are trusting him with your heart. It is a critical decision. That's why you must know his level of integrity—his willingness and ability to be honest and vulnerable in his core nature. Know his spiritual integrity and moral groundings.

This step is worth lingering over, for your ability to read and understand another's character will save you heartache down the road. I grew up hearing my father repeat an old proverb: If you can't know your jewels, know your jeweler. If you can't be sure of what your man is selling you, be sure you know his heart and his character.

What danger signs should you watch out for? Be wary of the person who...

- is inconsistent in his message
- is caught in deception

- pushes for physical intimacy without the emotional (and legal) commitment
- seems to dance around the topic of commitment
- pushes for commitment from you too quickly
- seems to lack healthy boundaries
- lacks a moral compass and solid moral behavior

Seventh, *if you sense something is wrong, it probably is.* While this counsel may not always be true, you will often develop a sense about whether a man is safe or he is playing you. Trust your hunches. Follow up on your uncomfortable feelings. Check them out with him, a trusted friend, or your pastor.

Finally, *cover all of your decisions in prayer and seek godly counsel.* The wise person makes decisions prayerfully. You must develop healthy decision-making skills, but you must also realize that we need God's wisdom to make good choices. That's why it is important for us to be quiet and listen—and not just to ourselves.

God's wisdom can often go against what we believe might be in our best interests. But as you draw close to God, He will influence you more and more in the most critical areas of your life.

Let It Simmer

Nothing is quite as good as a soup that has been left to simmer. I remember my mother's chicken broth—especially the wonderful aroma that wafted throughout the house the entire day. When I tried to sneak a sip before dinner, I received a scolding. "It's not soup yet," she would say. It sure looked like soup to me, but that was before I understood the importance of letting something simmer.

Likewise, you may be in a relationship that needs to simmer. And this isn't just an old wives' tale. Studies have confirmed the value of sleeping on important decisions. Perhaps you are involved in a new relationship that you are tempted to hurry along. But to do so would place unnecessary strain on you, him, and the relationship.

The more prudent course of action may be to let it simmer. If you have practiced the counsel in this chapter, sit back for a while and enjoy the ride. Assuming you have used your skills to discern his character and he has measured up, this may be the time to relax and let the relationship unfold naturally.

So double-check your ingredients, make sure the settings on your stove are right, and then relax—just let the relationship simmer. It will be soup soon enough, and the next step will come naturally.

SIX

YELLOW WARNING LIGHTS

If you are walking on the Decatur Road when winter turns to spring, you will probably slip and fall and hurt yourself. It is a mud-happy stretch at this turn, and if you are not careful you could very well slide all the way into Decatur.

JOE COOMER

Things are always changing. There is no such thing as safely coasting through life. We are either paying attention to the opportunities and dangers, or we are being swept along by circumstances—and that can be disastrous. We must keep an alert eye for warning lights to keep us on course. As we approach the intersections of life, including issues regarding relational commitment, we should keep an eye on the lights—the red one telling us to stop, the yellow ones indicating caution, and the green one telling us we can proceed.

In the last chapter, I shared that I was just a frothy sip away from joining forces in a coffee shop venture. I can't fully explain why coffee and coffee shops are so tantalizing to me, but they beckon like a far-off beacon to a lonely sailor. Whenever I see a new coffee shop, I simply must go in. Just hours ago, I visited a new spot in one of the suburbs of Seattle and found myself reenergized. The colors were rainbow-vibrant; the seating was inviting and hospitable. The owners acted as if I had been there a thousand times before, greeting me and asking about my travels. It was like a scene right out of *Cheers*.

So it is no surprise that I have been teased into possible ownership of such a place.

Community.

Conversation.

Comfort.

Creativity.

Soft music in the background, with a dollop of good taste thrown in. What could be better?

With this good taste on my tongue, I have been seriously tempted to venture into coffee company ownership. Not that I have a whit of business sense. But I do know coffee. And so about a month ago, I began to earnestly talk with an owner about partnering in her venture.

Things began with a heightened sense of excitement—about a vision, a dream, a possibility. This owner, Liz, was willing to take on a partner. Her shop had generated a lot of buzz in the community. (Pun intended!) The neighborhood needed a little sprucing up, the building was vacant and in desperate need of new ownership, and Liz had the vision to make it happen. What was once a dilapidated, empty eyesore is now an energetic gathering place. A bright red awning shades a lively, inviting logo of a man drinking his favorite cup of joe in the window.

Initial negotiations went well. Our "dating" proceeded smoothly. She liked me; I liked her. Our conversations were lively and enthusiastic. The initial price was right, but as I moved closer to her and began to engage in contract discussions, warnings appeared. The price of a partnership in the shop inched upward. Initial valuations doubled. The cost of doing business increased. I wondered what was happening.

As of this writing, Liz has been completely honest. But I have a churning sensation in my stomach as the business valuations have risen. I am mildly anxious, fretting about taking the final step into this deal. I have also found that my excitement is gone. The heady visions of a friendly neighborhood coffee shop have dissipated like so much steam off a latté. In its place are worries about the price of the partnership and my ability to afford such a venture.

Our relational dance has taken an awkward step off course. The movements are no longer smooth and effortless. I feel like a gangly adolescent in his first dance—and the feeling is enough to give me pause. It is a natural stage in any relationship—heeding the yellow caution lights on the way to making healthy commitments.

I must now take time to digest this turn in our relationship. I will ask questions:

- Why has the price of ownership increased in the past few weeks?
- Does she still want a partner, or is this her way of pushing me away?
- What is her commitment to our relationship?

These are important issues that we must deal with if the relationship is to be healthy.

Part of me wants to ignore the squeamish feelings in the pit of my stomach. Part of me wants to move steadfastly forward. Paying attention to warning signs is no fun. I do not enjoy dwelling on the possible loss of my dream.

Recently, a client named Sheila shared a similar dream—not about coffee, but about dancing with someone special and being embraced by an adoring suitor. Divorced nearly two years ago, she walked cautiously into my office, taking special notice of my degrees hanging on the wall. Her bland demeanor hinted at an underlying sadness.

During her first session, she told me that she has carefully constructed visions of love in her mind. She wanted me to assist her with the lingering feelings of discouragement at not finding Mr. Right. She wondered if she was doing something wrong.

Fifty years old and moderately overweight, Sheila was clearly unhappy about her physical appearance. She has yo-yo dieted with great frustration, and this served as a backdrop for her struggles. Though dressed sharply, this attractive woman has been discouraged in love and by love many times.

Sheila wondered aloud what she should do about Steve. With the first twinkle of excitement I had seen from her, she wondered aloud about the man she had been seeing for the past few months.

"I have some questions to ask you about him," she said. "I need professional advice about this situation."

"Please tell me about him," I offered. I had a hunch that she already knew the answers to some of her questions.

"Well, I met him at our singles' group at church. Steve is a nice guy, and I've enjoyed spending time with him. On the other hand, he told me that he's had two DUI convictions but still drinks. He smokes too. I try to tell myself that these things aren't a problem, but I'm not sure about that."

I watched as Sheila's eyes avoided mine, evidencing her discomfort.

"I like being with him," she offered enthusiastically. "He is a great conversationalist. I've really missed just having someone to talk to. I told him recently that I want to spend more time with him. I decided I was going to lay my feelings right out there."

"That was a stretch for you?" I asked.

"Definitely. I'm typically very cautious."

"So what happened?"

"He told me that he would really miss hanging out with me, but he didn't really want to spend more time with me. That he wasn't ready for any kind of commitment. That he has a busy life and couldn't fit a serious relationship into his schedule."

"How do you feel about that?"

"Well, I don't want to give up seeing him. But I wonder what you think."

Sheila smiled and looked out the window. Turning back to me she started to say something, then stopped.

"I think I already know what you're going to say," she said.

"Oh, really? You can read my mind? Maybe you already know what you think, and it's uncomfortable for you."

"Yup." She smiled and laughed.

"So, Sheila, I want to know what you think. You have undoubtedly given this a lot of thought. I'll bet you have Steve figured out pretty well."

I let my words sink in. I had a strong sense that Sheila knew she was seeing yellow warning lights and had mixed feelings about heeding them.

"You're probably going to tell me what my friends have already said and what I suspect."

Sheila seemed reluctant to share her perceptions. I sensed that she knew there were danger signals. Many times we avoid sharing the truth when it goes against our wishful feelings. On the other hand, perhaps she just needed me to confirm what her heart was already telling her.

"Well," she said softly. "He isn't ready to move forward with me. He wants to stay friends. And then there is the issue of his drinking. I try to ignore it, but I wonder if that could be a problem for us."

"I agree that you have reason to be cautious. He is clearly applying the brakes to your relationship. You had the courage to ask for more time with him and he said no. And he has shared some very big cautions about his history with alcohol—on top of the fact that he still drinks. These are major warning signs."

"This is exactly what my friends have told me. I was pretty sure I'd hear the same thing from you. I guess I need to give this some more thought. But finding a good guy is incredibly hard. I am so tired of looking for Mr. Right."

I could sense Sheila's struggle. She enjoyed spending time with Steve. He enjoyed spending time with her. They were having fun going to movies and hanging out. She risked sharing her feelings with him and was disappointed with his answer. He was not nearly as committed to her as she was to him!

Interested? Yes.

Willing to spend time with her? Yes.

Ready to move forward? No.

Perhaps you can relate to Sheila's plight. She is 50 and not especially self-confident. She wants a man in her life, but she also has standards. She senses danger but resists heeding it. She gets some good things from the relationship but risks a lot by continuing it. Sheila and I discussed the possibilities. Think them through with us.

She could disregard the warning signs about his alcohol use and his reluctance to get more involved. But by doing so, she will risk having her heart broken. She can move forward, caring about Steve more and more while prolonging the inevitable day of reckoning. Then, on that dreaded day, when she can no longer disregard his alcohol use and his unwillingness to fully commit, she will face monumental pain and feelings of rejection.

Or she can hope to can change his mind. She can believe that he will fall madly in love with her, pursue her with passion, and live happily ever after in her arms. In this fantasy, he quits drinking and seeks counseling for his alcohol abuse and resultant character problems.

Or she can enjoy the relationship for what it is. She can be honest with herself about his alcohol problems, smoking habit, and distancing maneuvers. She can decide that what he offers is enough for her—at least for now.

Her final option is to heed the warning signs and bid Steve adieu. She can thank him for the many wonderful evenings, the movies and dinners, and wish him well. She can see him at the singles meetings at their church and move on with her life, praying for new opportunities to meet a man who can truly satisfy her desires to be loved and respected.

The Value of Danger Signals

In my younger days, I had a lead foot. The Washington State Patrol and I were practically on a first-name basis for a while. Not that I am proud of such a distinction. But that's the way it was.

During one particularly bad spell, I was given multiple warnings for driving too fast. However, when this proved ineffective, the warnings stopped and the citations began. I was cited for speeding several times in one month. Each time I was annoyed because...well, because I was caught. I used all the rationalizations I could dream up. *Why aren't they out catching criminals? Why are they allowed to hide under bridges and behind embankments to catch us? Why do I have all the rotten luck?* But the truth of the matter was that I had been given plenty of warnings and had chosen to ignore them.

And then one day I received a letter that changed my life. It was the granddaddy of all warnings, the ultimate letter indicating how special I was. It said that I was invited (required) to participate in a special school for drivers like me, a sort of remedial driver's education class. I will never forget the ending: "Should you receive a ticket in the six months following your participation in this class, your driving privileges will be revoked."

It took me a moment to understand what this meant. *Driving privileges revoked?* This was serious. When I figured out that these folks meant business, I quickly decided that this would be the end of speeding for me. I was not going to risk losing my driving privilege. I took that letter and immediately taped it on the dashboard of my car. I looked at it every day and reminded myself that if I chose to speed, I would pay the consequences. And they would be stiff.

I am proud to say that I remained ticketless for many months. Long enough to get myself out of hot water. Long enough to lower my sky-high insurance premiums. Long enough to keep me sensitive to the speed limits since that time. Yes, I have slipped a bit a time or two, but I am now much more aware that cautions are in place for our benefit.

In previous chapters we talked about dangerous men. In fact, this book is largely about danger—how to avoid it, how to learn from it, and what to do about it once you have sensed that it is present in your love life. It is a matter of understanding that yellow caution lights are part of any commitment process. Warning signs, for you or for him, slow the process down until you can rectify problems. Warning signs tell us that we need to attend to something before moving forward.

Consider again Sheila's forewarnings about Steve. She had gained a lot of information in a very short time—and perhaps he was attending to some warning signs that he saw in her. Let's consider both possibilities.

Her yellow caution lights:

- his history of alcohol use
- his continued drinking
- his excuses for not spending more time with her
- his desire to be her "friend"

His possible yellow caution lights:

- her insistence on spending increasing time with him in spite of the boundaries he had set
- her excessive dependence
- her self-esteem issues

Both had received significant warning indicators that they needed to attend to. The signs were there for their benefit. Whether or not they chose to heed them was another matter.

God's Warnings

The Scriptures are filled with yellow caution lights. God doesn't use these warnings to spoil all our fun but to increase our safety and joy. They don't come from an angry, vengeful God but from a loving Father who is looking out for our welfare.

Consider the warning lights in Luke 12. Jesus is warning His disciples about the Pharisees—the so-called religious leaders of the day. He knows the deceitful hearts of the Pharisees and sees the contradictions between their actions and their role as religious leaders.

"Be on your guard against the yeast of the Pharisees, which is hypocrisy. There is nothing concealed that will not be disclosed, or hidden that will not be made known" (Luke 12:1-2). Another translation reads: "More than anything else, beware of these Pharisees and the way they pretend to be good when they aren't. But such hypocrisy cannot be hidden forever. It will become evident as yeast in dough" (TLB).

In other passages, Jesus again protests the hypocrisy of the Pharisees. He says of them, "You are like whitewashed tombs, which look beautiful on the outside but on the inside are full of dead men's bones and everything unclean. In the same way, on the outside you appear to people as righteous but on the inside you are full of hypocrisy and wickedness" (Matthew 23:27-28).

Although this passage clearly contains a warning to the disciples concerning the Pharisees, it also has valuable lessons for us. Let's reflect on some of the lessons in this passage and what they might say about warnings related to the pursuit of a committed relationship.

First, *Jesus knows the hearts of humankind regardless of what people look like on the outside.* Men may be crafty and deceptive, but Jesus knows what is truly taking place in their hearts. Because you have the heart and mind of Christ, you too can sense and understand what is occurring in the heart and mind of your man. Your spirit can determine when something is amiss.

The apostle Paul prays for the church at Ephesus a prayer of power and wisdom that could be very helpful to you.

> I keep asking that the God of our Lord Jesus Christ, the glorious Father, may give you the Spirit of wisdom and revelation, so that you may know him better. I pray also that the eyes of your heart may be enlightened in order that you may know the hope to which he has called you, the riches of his glorious inheritance in the saints, and his incomparably great power for us who believe. That power is like the working of his mighty strength, which he exerted in Christ when he raised him from the dead and seated him at his right hand in the heavenly realms, far above all rule and authority, power and dominion, and every title that can be given, not only in the present age but also in the one to come (Ephesians 1:17-21).

What a wonderful gift we have as Christians—the gift of the Holy Spirit and accompanying wisdom. The Holy Spirit will tell us, if we listen, when we are approaching danger.

Second, *be cautious of anyone who pretends to be too good.* Hypocrisy abounded in Jesus' day, and it is alive and well in our world as well. We must be careful of anyone who is too quick to promote himself or his image. This is manipulation. In reference to the

Pharisees, Jesus called it a whitewash. Although you may want to see the man in your life as Mr. Wonderful, take a moment to look for the wrinkles and blemishes because they are there. If you resist checking him out, you may want to ask yourself what you are afraid of finding.

Third, *everything will be revealed in time.* Deception and troublesome traits cannot hide indefinitely. They will rise to the surface for all to see—assuming we are willing to look, as Jesus instructs us to do. Negative traits can be hidden for a season, but in time they will surface.

This last truth is a good reason to take your time when dating someone. I cannot tell you how many problems have occurred because someone has "fallen in love," gotten engaged, and married—all within six months. (Some of you may be squirming.) Although we all know of exceptions to the rule, you should take a reasonable amount of time to truly get to know someone before you commit your life and love to him. Make sure that you have seen him in his good times and bad and know the shadow side of his personality.

Character Problems

I commonly counsel clients about character problems. Character problems often surface when couples face issues of commitment and intimacy.

I teach my clients to look at people's character and what might cause problems down the line. What qualities will make someone safe and nurturing for you to be around, and conversely, what qualities will make life difficult for you? I have helped many women consider character traits in men that may raise red flags (or at least yellow caution lights) regarding intimacy and commitment.

Sam Shepherd provides a good definition of character in the *21st Century Dictionary of Quotations*: "Character is an essential tendency. It can be covered up, it can be messed with, it can be screwed around with, but it can't be ultimately changed. It's like the structure of our bones, the blood that runs through our veins."[1]

Short of a life-changing, heart-changing conversion experience or in-depth counseling, we are like zebras whose stripes are not likely to be changed. That can be good news or bad, depending on the issue at hand.

Let's consider the implications of character, keeping in mind that problematic character traits ought to serve as blinking yellow lights to you. Or if you have the misfortune of a past association with the Washington State Patrol, these might be more like an alternating series of flashing red and blue lights instructing you to pull over and be prepared to show your driver's license. And be prepared to either change or pay the piper as well.

To help us understand the implications of character problems, we'll examine several scenarios that offer character warning lights. These are questions that both women and men may ask when they consider intimacy and commitment in their relationships.

What if I am with a man who doesn't share his feelings? As much as you may try to deny it, this is a character problem. Many things can keep a man from learning to share his feelings, as I discuss in my book *Does Your Man Have the Blues?* Many men are closed down, shut off from their feelings, and they have been this way for many years. Of course this creates a significant barrier to effective communication and healthy relating. Without rigorous counseling, relational training, and spiritual intervention, this character problem is not likely to change readily. Conversely, with counseling, the reading of good relationship material, and spiritual help, change is possible.

What if my man has a history of substance abuse but contends that this is just recreational and insists that it is not a problem? This is the big D—denial (not to be confused with the river in Egypt). It also stands for Danger. Any kind of drug use or alcohol abuse will lead to character problems. In my experience, most substance abuse leads to irritability, self-centeredness, lack of motivation, deception, and inevitable relationship problems. Substance abuse is also almost always a symptom of deeper problems.

What if my man says he wants to keep seeing me while seeing other women as well? Obviously, this man doesn't want to commit to a relationship. He wants to play the field, and you will need to decide if this is what you are after in a relationship. Don't expect him to change his attitude anytime soon. If you are looking for a committed relationship, his insistence on having other women in his life is a giant warning sign.

What if the man I am seeing cannot own up to problems—he always has someone else to blame? This is a character problem we often see with narcissistic individuals. These individuals frequently have problems with their conscience, rarely allowing themselves to feel badly for hurting others or to say those wonderful relational words, "I'm sorry." When you try to pin these men down, they dodge, change the subject, and generally make you feel kind of crazy. Without the ability to take responsibility for their problems or make amends for them, they cannot resolve conflict in a healthy way.

What if my husband can't stay away from his mother and father? Taken literally, assuming that this man cannot let go of his parents as we are instructed to do in the book of Genesis, this is a significant character problem of dependence. We are encouraged to leave our parents and cleave to our mate, and a failure to make this break indicates an excessive dependency and enmeshment with his parents. He will need to face this problem and work to develop a healthier sense of relatedness to them. Ideally a couple will work together to determine the right amount of contact.

What if the man I am dating always seems to create conflict? Unfortunately, this is a classic character problem. Many individuals seem to thrive on conflict, as much as they might say that they hate it. They live in ambivalence; they live in contradiction; they cannot seem to give or live one coherent message.

This obviously creates intense conflict for the partner as well. You cannot be around someone who creates conflict without feeling at least some of that conflict yourself.

Steven Carter and Julia Sokol, in their book *He's Scared, She's Scared,* share their perspective on conflict in relationships. "No matter how much these men and women claim to want an easy, uncomplicated love relationship, on some level they are always creating conflict. These men and women will usually be giving their partners a wide variety of intense messages that can best be described as mixed or double." For example, they may be...

- very seductive but very rejective
- very intimate but very withdrawn
- very accepting but very critical
- very tender but very hostile
- very romantic but very distant
- very sexually provocative but very sexually withholding
- very giving but very cold

"This behavior is very confusing at best," say Carter and Sokol, "whether you are on the receiving end or you are the one acting it out."[2]

Carter and Sokol say many people simply have not learned how to fight in a healthy way. They have not learned how to create healthy distance when they need it and may use fighting as a way to obtain space from one another.

What if I am dating a man who I believe has core character problems? If any of the above scenarios fit you or your man, you need professional help. Only rarely can people change character problems without assistance. We don't usually see how we act out our character problems. Most often, we deny, minimize, and rationalize away our character issues, causing problems for others in our lives. We need professional help in order to make significant change.

The Problem with Change

If you are married to or dating someone with significant character problems—to the point that the yellow warning lights are turning your blue blouse a hazy shade of green—the situation is not hopeless. It is, however, serious. You must decide to take things seriously if you want change.

Judy came to see me with her husband, Dan. Both said that they wanted a greater degree of intimacy in their marriage and wanted help to attain their goals.

Judy and Dan were both 30 years old and had two young children. Dan worked in the telecommunications field, making adjustments to communication towers. Judy worked as a marketing advisor for a large steel manufacturing company. Both worked long, hard hours, and balancing their professional lives with their marriage and family life had become a primary issue.

Judy and Dan stated that they felt unhappy with one another and believed that their intimacy was suffering, primarily because of their busy schedules. As I explored this issue further with them, both indicated unhappiness with this busyness and emotional distance between them, and both wanted to bridge the gap.

But as I explored their marital history, I quickly discovered that the distance between them—physical, emotional, and spiritual—had existed for years. They were investing a great deal of energy into their careers and children with little left for each other. Although they maintained a superficial commitment to one another, they had failed to sit down and truly review the status of their marriage. The bottom line was that they had never made a conscious decision to commit more time and energy to their relationship. Subsequently, they were living in a loveless, lifeless marriage—lacking of the relational zest they desired.

Judy and Dan told me that they had experienced a scare recently when she, while away on a business trip, nearly had an affair. Judy came home from her trip feeling guilty and immediately told Dan of her experience. She expressed a desire to obtain counseling, and he readily agreed.

As we explored their history, we could see the warning signs they had previously ignored:

- being too busy to do special things with one another
- taking one another for granted
- creating friendships with the opposite sex
- spending more time away from home
- putting increasing energy into their work
- attending church irregularly

We determined that they had a lot of work to do. They had obvious issues with commitment—not the kind we have discussed in dating situations, but a much different kind—that are frequently found in marriages. Dan and Judy had a legal commitment to one another but not an emotional one. Both needed to recommit themselves to creating a vibrant marriage, making it eventful and exciting.

They could no longer put all of their energies into their work and children. Their marriage needed an infusion of energy, life, and passion. Each had to take responsibility for being a fun and interesting mate—listening to one another and being committed to showing an interest in each other. They also agreed to set healthy boundaries on relationships with the opposite sex, keeping a safe distance so that unhealthy attachments did not take place. They did not want to take any chances on any problems in this area in the future.

Some of Dan and Judy's work involved character adjustment. And in their case, cosmetic change was not enough. They had to heed the warning signs and decide to commit to deep transformation. This involved reading material on marriage enrichment, communication, and intimacy. It involved painstaking analysis of old patterns of behavior that they needed to eliminate or modify. Fortunately, both were motivated to do the necessary work. They counted the cost of change and agreed their marriage was worth the effort.

Dan and Judy dodged a bullet, and their marriage is stronger today than it was when I first met them. Although they still have work to do, they are on their way to significant character and marital change.

Screening for Trouble

Learning to screen for trouble by being observant of yellow warning lights can be invaluable. But I am surprised to see how few people have perfected this skill.

Drs. Barry Lubetkin and Elena Oumano, in their book *Bailing Out*, offer some insightful questions to keep on hand as you navigate your relationship. Although their questions are designed primarily for those in a dating relationship, they can be helpful for marital partners as well. Lubetkin and Oumano explain why screening is important:

> You can screen at any stage of a relationship. It is hoped that you will begin the process of observing or querying the following areas of concern early on—before you commit—to accumulate the information you need to make a reasonable, objective judgment as to whether the relationship will succeed or fail…Screening will provide you with a detailed fund of information about your partner upon which you can make a more reasoned, objective decision. Another important reason for learning to screen now is that you will be more confident of your ability to choose more wisely in the future.[3]

They suggest asking these questions:

- What does the person share with you about his past relationships?
- How long did these relationships last?
- Were they monogamous?
- How many relationships or marriages has he had?
- Did he take breaks between relationships, or was he unable to handle being alone?
- What made him move into the next relationship?
- What caused past relationships to end? Boredom? Infidelity? Addictions?
- What kind of incompatibilities existed?

The authors emphasize that he should be able and willing to answer these questions, and of course his answers are worthy of critical review. Each question delves into important areas, offering potential yellow warning lights. You should be willing to explore each area, using wisdom to consider his answers.

If he gets defensive, you need to ask why. If he has not considered these questions, this too is a source of concern. Hopefully, he will be willing to explore these issues with you. If not, you should be seeing a big, yellow caution light!

Moving Past the Warning Lights

Thankfully, we don't always have to look in our rearview mirror or scan the horizon for warning lights. We do not need to be paralyzed by fear. However, we must be determined to deal with these warning signs and then move forward.

Sheila spent several months in counseling and learned some difficult lessons. She stayed with Steve longer than she thought best before finally saying goodbye. But in the process she learned to trust herself, God, and the yellow caution lights. She decided she wanted to be with someone who wanted to spend more time and energy with her. She is wiser, stronger, healthier, and better prepared for a more positive relationship. And now that she is ready, the right man may be ready for her.

Many men are able to move beyond the warning lights and the troubling behavior that accompanies them. They are finally able to take the necessary steps on the path to responsible adult commitment.

Take inventory of your relationship. Are you in a legally committed marriage but lacking the vibrancy and warmth that God intended? You may need to lovingly confront your man and explain that you need more from him.

Perhaps you are actively dating after a disappointing divorce, but you keep being blindsided by problems. You can learn from the past and move beyond the warning signs. You have already taken the first step by picking up this book in your search for answers. You are ready to move forward.

Take the time to heed and analyze the yellow warning lights in your life to determine their meaning. Every problem has an answer—but to reach an effective solution, you must first analyze the problem accurately.

Remember, God has given you His wisdom in these matters, and He will not fail you. After analyzing the caution lights, you may realize that your next step requires action.

Be bold. You are capable of making changes that will help you enjoy an emotionally and physically committed relationship in the future.

SEVEN

THE REAL NATURE OF COMMITMENT

He who would see himself clearly must open up to a confidant freely chosen and worthy of such trust.

DR. PAUL TOURNIER

Commitment is a willingness to write another person indelibly into your future. It means selling yourself out—no holds barred, no backdoor exits. It means saying, "I'm in this for the duration and willing to do anything to make the relationship thrive." That is what commitment is all about. And that is what you must expect from yourself and your man if you are to enjoy a fully developed relationship.

This kind of commitment is priceless because it is not easy to come by. But you already know that. You understand that the monster of commitment phobia can rear its ugly head in many ways. You are also aware that many people say they are committed to someone or something but then act as if they had their fingers crossed behind their back. They are committed for a week or two. They are committed until a better deal comes along. Or perhaps they are committed but fail to see the troubling character traits that will bring the relationship crashing down.

Perhaps you and your man are willing to remain committed to one another but far less willing to practice emotional transparency. This, as we all know, is not full commitment. It may mean caring, it may mean strong affection, it may even mean love, but it does not equate to commitment. Commitment includes the willingness to immerse yourself physically, emotionally, and spiritually in the relationship.

These truths took on new meaning for me when I was divorced several years ago. It was, without question, the most painful experience of my life. Adam called Eve "bone of my bones and flesh of my flesh," and when that flesh was torn from me, the rip was agonizing. It should be agonizing.

I did not want the divorce, and at times I could hardly place one foot in front of the other. I seriously questioned whether God could have any use for me, whether my ministry was washed up, and whether I would lose many of my lifetime friends. I dreaded possible rejection from the church. In short, I was an emotional wreck.

Time and God's grace have provided healing. Hundreds of phone calls to my parents, who have functioned as literal godsends, saved me from despair. Friends loved and nurtured me through the ordeal, and I found sanctuary within the church, where I received comfort and support.

Now, some years later, as I write this book about commitment, I realize the issues meant for the reader also fit the author. I have had to struggle anew with issues of commitment in my current relationship. And no wonder—as they say, once bitten, twice shy.

During the healing process, at a time when up looked like down and down looked like up, I reassessed my life. I realized that I needed some new inner and outer landscaping. I decided a bed-and-breakfast on the saltwater might be in my future. I have always dreamed of creating a special place for people who, like me, need to get away long enough to renew, reinvigorate, and restore their weary spirits. I know the power of a kind word and gentle voice, set against the backdrop of God's magnificent creation. I felt the inexorable draw to create such a place for others.

A few years ago I purchased a piece of property that, as they say, had my name on it. Dense with fir, cedar and madrone trees that clung together precariously high on a ridge with a sweeping view of Hood Canal and the snow-capped Olympic Mountains, it was a place where I sensed God's presence. Right there—right in the middle of this verdant refuge of creation, overlooking the only fjord in the United States, I prayed for a special blessing and was eventually able to purchase it.

And then I met Christie. It all started simply enough—a movie and dinner. But I found that I had to see her again, and again. Yes, she is special, and yes, she brought joy back into my life. Oh, I know all that stuff about being complete as an individual, but I'll take a genuine relationship any day. A burnt orange Olympic sunset is always sweeter when you share it with someone you care about. She shared my faith, my love of nature, and, incredibly, my dream of owning a bed-and-breakfast.

Our early dating life was delightful. Christie loves color, design, houses, family, and all things spiritual. She makes me think about life in new ways, challenging me to be more tolerant and forgiving—and to have fun.

All was fine for a while, but then *it* began to sink in. Real commitment includes closing the back doors. It means blocking or locking the exits. Was I ready for this?

Here I was writing a book on commitment, and I found that my writing was hitting me squarely between the eyes. I hadn't bargained for this. Perhaps it was time to call my publisher and ask him to reconsider the project.

I had issues to face. Was I willing to share my bed-and-breakfast dream with her? Was I willing to write her into my future? Was I willing to consider the big C—commitment? I had to determine just how much I cared about her and whether I was willing to move through the stages of commitment with her—from not yet being ready, counting the cost of commitment, preparing myself for commitment, using the dynamics of our relationship as the means where I would commit myself to her and, finally, learning to cherish the commitment. Was I willing to face my fears about our moving through these stages to ultimate commitment to her?

Another change occurred that put the damper on my bed-and-breakfast dream. Trouble was brewing at the OK Corral. Not everyone on the Kitsap Peninsula was excited about the arrival of a bed-and-breakfast. An errant e-mail had found its way into my hands. The message indicated that some folks were opposed to my venture. This news surprised me. Who would not want something as magical as a bed-and-breakfast in their neighborhood? Well, one Norwegian family that had lived in the area for many years, for starters. Their acerbic tone suggested more than mild displeasure.

Part of the application process for a bed-and-breakfast includes taking out an ad in the local paper, indicating that you are planning to build a bed-and-breakfast next door. The ad also invites these friends and neighbors to complain if they are not as excited about the project as you are.

As of this writing, Christie and I are deliberating how committed we are to this venture, as more than a handful of neighborly folks do not want it to transpire. We must decide what lengths we are willing to go to in order to make it happen. And, in the meantime, we are talking about us and the future.

Both the bed-and-breakfast and Christie will require a great deal of commitment and will demand energy, courage, and tenacity, as well as legal and emotional actions demonstrating that commitment.

Mere words will not be enough to win Christie's heart or navigate the hurdles to make the bed-and-breakfast a reality. But if either commitment is halfhearted, that means I lack the necessary ingredients to make them happen. I am convinced that the struggle will make the journey worth the effort.

The Anatomy of Commitment

Writing someone into our future is part and parcel of this thing called commitment. It includes both legal and emotional unions. One without the other is vapid. To make a legal pledge to your beloved and then fail to share the intimate details of your life is unacceptable. The relationship cannot be sustained. To make an emotional commitment to your beloved but refuse to write him or her into your future is equally insipid.

What are the pieces of a wholehearted commitment? What does a full, vibrant commitment look like? Consider these elements of the deeply committed relationship—one to which you can aspire and one that you can expect from your loved one.

A Vow

Committed partners have made a vow to one another. This vow is a binding, covenantal relationship, similar to the one God makes with us. He binds His heart to ours, and we are His children. In marriage, or in the premarital relationship, each vows to belong exclusively to the other. No others are invited into this sacred space. The boundaries shout to others, "Stay out! She is mine. We belong to each other." Just as God is fiercely jealous for our hearts, we are fiercely jealous for the heart of our mate. And this is how it should be.

Certainly this exclusive relationship includes freedom to develop aspects of your personality. This vow of exclusivity is not meant to be stifling; in fact, it is freeing. The boundaries create safety and freedom from feelings of abandonment that arise in the temporary or nonexclusive relationship. Like children in a fenced yard, committed couples have plenty of room to play and explore, but they agree to stay within the prescribed and accepted limits.

No Others

Within this exclusive, committed relationship, each agrees to give up pursuing other romantic interests. Here is the letting go of other options, which creates tension for those who are not ready to be fenced in. But most people realize that at some point the endless search for the elusive perfect mate must end, and we get down to the business of creating fullness in our relationship. Right here, and nowhere else, we can create richness in relationships.

Judith Viorst talks about this in her book *Grown-Up Marriage:*

> The women of my generation were looking for lifetime, not slice-of-life, companions. We were looking for a strings-and-rings relationship. We wanted to know, for the next fifty years, exactly who our New Year's Eve date would be. We wanted to be not semi, but totally married…The point of the covenant marriage is to lock in forever and throw away the key.[1]

Lest we feel as if we are giving up so much by relinquishing other options—the great fear of so many commitment-phobes—we must remind ourselves of the truth of the matter. Professor Linda Waite, director of the Marriage Project at the Institute of Family Values, notes in *The Case for Marriage,* "We have looked at well over 1,000 studies that overwhelmingly show the strong and consistent relationship between marriage and well-being."[2] She and colleague Marie Gallagher found that married couples seem to be blessed with better sex, greater happiness, longer lives, shorter hospital stays, more money, and less anxiety and depression than cohabitating couples. They seem to live more settled lives and have happier children and better health. So much for greener grass on the other side!

Transparency

There is transparency in the committed relationship. In John Powell's simple and delightful bestselling book, *Why Am I Afraid to Tell You Who I Am?* he talks about the different stages of relating. He explains how we move from superficial, clichéd conversation to gut-level communication where we share our thoughts, attitudes, and feelings. Gut-level communication provides tremendous healing, but unfortunately, it does not take place in many relationships. Safety is required to talk on this level.[3]

Powell correctly notes that we are often afraid to be honest with one another. We erect social conventions—politeness, posturing, and head games—in order to avoid sharing our true feelings with one another. Covenantal, committed marriage affords us a safe place where we can be transparent with one another. In this haven, where we have some assurance that our mate will not pack up and leave, we can share our thoughts and feelings.

You may be in a legally or emotionally committed relationship and still lack this gut-level communication that Powell refers to. You may have settled for a dance of distance, a familiarity without feelings, an understanding without excitement. I suggest, and I think Powell would agree, that deep, gut-level communication is not taking place in relationships that have too much caution and not enough risk. With practice and the expectation that sharing will occur, real communication can take place.

I offer a simple exercise here to help you move your relationship toward emotional transparency:

Encourage your mate to sit down with you every evening for ten minutes. Pick a topic. Take turns sharing how you feel and what you want. Your mate must listen and reflect his understanding. Then switch places and have your mate try the same thing. Remember, agreement is not critical. The goal is to understand and accept your partner's point of view.

Tension

The committed relationship tolerates tension. Yes, tension is a part of a blissful marriage as well as a premarital committed relationship. The relationship has room for tension to exist, but those in a committed relationship know they will resolve the tension. They feel safe knowing that both will return to the heated issue and find resolution. The tension is not enough to break the bonds that hold the partners together. Nothing can sever their bonds of love, and together they will solve the problem.

I feel assured that Christie and I will find the solution to our bed-and-breakfast difficulties. We do not yet know how we will resolve them—we only know that we are locking arms as we move forward. We are utilizing gut-level, honest communication with one another. This offers me great peace and real connection to her. She stands with me in finding the solution to our problems. She stands with me in making plans to talk with our disgruntled neighbors. She stands with me.

Support

The partners in a committed relationship support one another in good times and bad. This is one of the great beauties of the committed relationship. We can much more easily tolerate the many storms that come our way when we are buoyed by loved ones who let us know they are with us regardless of what we face.

I want to share again the powerful influence my parents had on me during my heartbreaking divorce. Words cannot explain the gratitude I felt knowing that I could pick up the phone and call them at any time, day or night, when I was in a funk. Whenever

I feared my heart would break, my parents comforted me and held me in their hearts.

I distinctly remember them saying, "Son, we don't know what to do for you. We feel so helpless. But if you will talk to us, we'll listen. We love you." That was more than enough.

Last night at our family's pre-Mother's Day gathering, I looked around at my extended family. My brother John and his wife, Joanne, and their grown children. Tammy and Rick, their mates, and their children; my sisters, Shar and Sue, and their mates. It gave me a wonderful sense of belonging. They too spent time on the phone with me in good times and bad. They know me—my likes, dislikes, and foibles. And I offer them support whenever I can. I am interested in what happens in their lives, and together we create a web of caring.

Now I am blessed once again to have a special, loving person in my life who recognizes when I am feeling low and need a kind word. And Christie knows that I am available to her when she faces difficulties as well. Committed relationships provide safe harbor from the tumultuous storms of life.

More on Gut-Level Communication

Because gut-level communication is a significant piece of the fully committed relationship, we would do well to learn more about it. Again I am indebted to John Powell's wonderful primer on the subject, *Why Am I Afraid to Tell You Who I Am?* If we can envision honest, loving communication, perhaps we can come a bit closer to emulating it in our primary relationships.

Powell describes five levels of communication, ranking from least transparent to most intimate.

The fifth level is *cliché conversation,* the lowest level of self-communication. Here, we talk in clichés—"How are you?" or "I'm glad it's sunny today." Powell says, "This is the conversation, the non-communication, of the cocktail party, the club meeting, the neighborhood laundromat, etc. There is no sharing of persons at all."[4] Such conversation is often appealing because it is safe.

The fourth level is *reporting the facts about others*. Obviously, we commonly spend time on this level. We can easily gossip about people or share an opinion about them. By focusing on others, we are required to share very little about ourselves. We risk the minimum and gain the minimum as well.

The third level is *my ideas and judgments*. Here, we are willing to risk telling others some of our ideas and revealing some of our judgments. However, we remain guarded and want to be sure that those ideas and judgments will be accepted before we share more.

The second level is *my feelings*. After sharing our ideas and judgments, we can still reveal a lot more. We can share how we feel about those same ideas and judgments. We can share how a particular event makes us feel. If we fail to move beyond sharing ideas and judgments, Powell says, the conversation will be stifled. This stunted communication suggests that we have little commitment to true intimacy in the relationship. Conversely, sharing our feelings makes the conversation more personal, intimate, and risky.

The first level is *peak communication*. This is our goal in the committed relationship. Powell says, "All deep and authentic friendships, and especially the union of those who are married, must be based on absolute openness and honesty. At times, gut-level communication will be most difficult, but it is at these precise times that it is most necessary."[5]

Powell is quick to point out that we cannot spend all of our time on this level. Not every interaction can or should be peak communication. But there need to be moments when we will feel completely at ease, willing to share whatever is important to us. We must also be willing to listen to the other person completely and unconditionally.

If God Is For Us

Our relationships with one another are, of course, human. We will ultimately disappoint each other because of human limitations. Consider some stark facts about human nature:

- We are prone to dishonesty.
- We are prone to disloyalty.
- We are prone to selfishness.
- We are prone to aggression.
- We are prone to passive-aggressiveness.
- We are prone to secrecy.
- We are prone to childish behavior.
- We are prone to addictive and compulsive behaviors.

Given this discouraging array of troublesome traits, we might wonder how we can keep a relationship moving forward at all. But, thank God, He is the antithesis of the above traits. Consider Christ:

- He is honest and abides in the truth.
- He is knowable and relational.
- He is loyal and devoted to us.
- He is not puffed up with His attributes.
- He is gentle and kind.
- He is open and sincere.
- He is our Abba Father.
- He has no addictions or compulsions.

Jesus Christ is in love with us. He provides the perfect model of the committed relationship. A passage in Romans gives us a glimpse of His love and offers us hope:

> And we know that in all things God works for the good of those who love him, who have been called according

to his purpose. For those God foreknew he also predestined to be conformed to the likeness of his Son, that he might be the firstborn among many brothers. And those he predestined, he also called; those he called, he also justified; those he justified, he also glorified. What, then, shall we say in response to this? If God is for us, who can be against us? (Romans 8:28-31).

Many people have looked to this famous passage to assuage painful feelings. I know that I have hidden myself in verse 28 when things were rough. I was confident of my love for God and comforted myself in His love for me. I was certain that everything would work out regardless of how dark things looked at the moment.

As comforting as these words are, they are not the sum of this passage. There is more for us to consider.

Who are the recipients of this promise? Paul says it is those who have been *called according to his purpose*. Here is the height of divine commitment. God knows all. He is the first and the last, the Alpha and Omega, the beginning and the end (Revelation 1:8). We are able to respond to Him because He first made a way for us to do so. That is commitment!

God is the author of relational commitment. Each and every trait listed above concerning commitment is found in Him. He is knowable, relational, loving, and loyal, and He cares about the tiniest details of our lives. He intimately understands our sufferings and can identify with us in them. His heart grieves when we grieve.

This brief passage ends with a powerful line, one that is worthy of our meditations. "If God is for us, who can be against us?" To me, this means that I can let out a big sigh. Everything that comes into my life has first been strained through God's hands. He is allowing things to unfold in my life and can use it all to His glory and for my benefit. I can rest in knowing that He is completely committed to me.

Paul asks, "What, then, shall we say in response to this?" How about "Thank You, Lord, for choosing me to be in a committed, safe, and wonderful relationship with You!"

Or perhaps we can echo the words of John: "You are worthy, our Lord and God, to receive glory and honor and power, for you created all things, and by your will they were created and have their being" (Revelation 4:11).

Holy Listening

Something deeply spiritual and tremendously exciting can take place in a fully developed relationship. We experience one of the highest forms of love when we listen to and understand each other. In a safe, committed relationship, we can share not only our deepest hurts and most treasured aspirations but also those things that are holy and spiritual to us. This is a most poignant aspect of commitment—that we agree to act as holy listeners to our mates.

Holy listening is not common. It is part of the contemplative tradition, which values silence and quietude and where people walk softly alongside others as they search to define and describe their relationship to God.

In this special place, you act as a midwife to the yearnings of your mate's soul. You help him verbalize what God is saying to him. The apostle Paul used the language of birth to describe our search for God: "We know that the whole creation has been groaning as in the pains of childbirth right up to the present time. Not only so, but we ourselves, who have the firstfruits of the Spirit, groan inwardly as we wait eagerly for our adoption as sons, the redemption of our bodies" (Romans 8:22-23).

As a holy listener to your mate, you have the opportunity to be a spiritual midwife. You have the opportunity to pay special attention to what he is saying and what he is not saying. You might listen for the subtleties of your partner's language. How does he talk about his relationship with God? What are his frustrations as he walks the path of being a Christian? What does he deeply desire from God? These are several questions you can encourage your mate to talk with you about as well.

Margaret Guenther, in her book *Holy Listening*, talks about the importance of listening:

> *Listen* is such a little, ordinary word that it is easily passed over. Yet we all know the pain of not being listened to, of not being heard. I feel a clutch at my heart whenever I see a child who is desperate, inarticulate with grief, crying for his preoccupied parent to listen to him. My vicarious anguish seems excessive until I realize that I am that child fearing the awful emptiness when a voice goes unheard.[6]

How much are you and I like the child who longs to be heard? Who is more fitting to really hear us now than our partner? As you refine the special skill of holy listening, you will most certainly grow in your relationship and commitment to your mate.

The Three Dailies

Sometimes commitment may feel like an awfully big bite to take. I must admit that at times, the big C feels overwhelming until I break it down into some very real practicalities. Commitment and emotional intimacy, the backbone of this book, can be simplified by following what Douglas Weiss calls "the three dailies" in his book *Intimacy*. Weiss recommends making the following practice part of your relationship. If you are striving toward a committed relationship with your spouse, add these components to your daily ritual.

Prayer

Weiss insists that prayer is an absolute necessity in your relationship. He says, "I am constantly amazed when couples tell me that the last time they really prayed together, not including praying over food or a good night prayer with children, was years ago. Sometimes they say, 'We both pray, just not together.'"[7]

David offers some important counsel in Psalm 127:1: "Unless the LORD builds the house, its builders labor in vain." This points out that including the Lord in the building of your relationship is critical. Needless to say, you should include this aspect in the beginning of your relationship because adding it later may be awkward and difficult.

Christie and I have added prayer to our lives. As we consider the seriousness of a committed life together, we want the Lord to be an integral part of our relationship. Even as I pray for our future, I also pray that the Lord will reveal any difficulties that may need our attention prior to moving forward in our relationship. I have found prayer to be such a critical aspect of keeping our hearts right and for gaining wisdom.

Feelings

Weiss says that emotional intimacy is the second very important aspect that couples need to develop and maintain throughout their relationship. I agree. This is an integral part of gut-level communication. But it takes practice. And as the saying goes, practice does *not* make perfect; perfect practice makes perfect. What does perfect practice look like?

Sharing emotions with one another requires having respect for your partner's feelings even though you may not agree with him. Emotions are such a central part of who we are that we must treat them as sacred territory. You will need to practice sharing your feelings and asking your mate to share his. Don't be discouraged if your mate struggles to identify and share his feelings. This skill will come in time and with practice.

Here is an exercise I use with couples as they practice sharing the language of feelings. Try it and see how it works for you.

> I feel _____ when you _____. I would really appreciate it if you would _____.

Here is an example: "Steve, I feel lonely when you stay late at the office. I would really appreciate it if you would commit to coming home at least three evenings a week to share dinner with me and the kids."

Here's another example: "Honey, you criticize me so often that it drags me down. I would appreciate it if you would remember to build me up at times for the things I'm doing right. I need more encouragement right now."

Weiss shares an important insight from his counseling experience: "In a marriage in which a spouse feels emotionally unsafe, over time the partner will choose to stop being emotionally intimate."[8] You must make a practice of sharing your emotions and helping your man feel safe to do so.

Praise and Nurturing

The third daily practice Weiss recommends is praise and nurturing. These are essential ingredients for a vibrant, ongoing intimate relationship.

Who does not like to be around someone who champions them? Most of us feel as if we did not receive the affirmation we needed growing up and have a big empty place inside where we are desperate for encouragement. When I talk to couples about how often they encourage one another, I am often met with blank stares. Some people never consider that their partner might be starved for affection. And I truly mean starved. Tragically, when people do not receive affirmation in the relationship, they may look elsewhere for it.

Weiss offers an exercise that is helpful to learning this critical aspect of commitment. First, you each think of two things you love, appreciate, or value about each other. You share yours with your mate while he listens and acknowledges your observations. Then you switch roles—your mate says two things that he values or appreciates about you. Practicing this exercise will help you make a habit of praising and appreciating one another.

The Imperfect Path of Commitment

Although we can learn many skills to help us navigate the journey, there is no perfect path to commitment. You must be careful to set the goal of commitment clearly before you while also keeping one foot firmly planted in reality. We are people, and that means we are imperfect. And we are all in process.

Be careful about your expectations. We can easily move from one extreme to another. If we experience disappointment, we may shift from expecting someone to be totally and completely committed to us to believing that no one can be trusted or give anything to us. We go from believing that we ought to be able to find someone who can give us everything to believing that no one will ever meet any of our needs. This type of black-and-white thinking carries obvious dangers.

This dance of commitment is an imperfect one. The music changes, and we must be light on our feet. More specifically, you will do well to acknowledge that you may run into men who cannot possibly give you a commitment or who are incapable of providing any emotional transparency. More often, however, you will find a man in process, one who can give you some things but not others. Perhaps he will be good at creating a physical commitment to you but will need to work on his emotional involvement. Your path to commitment will be easy and painless in some places, difficult and challenging in others. Be prepared to encounter shades of gray on the path.

As I write this book I am learning a great deal about commitment as I work things out in my relationship with Christie. It is here—as I practice trusting, sharing, and writing her into my life and future—that the real learning is being done. I read a little, pray a little, share a little, and learn a lot. I practice sharing my fears and emotions with Christie, step-by-step.

I also observe where she is on the path to commitment. What are our strengths? What are our weaknesses? And are we willing to work together to deal with the problems we each bring to the relationship? I am practicing holy listening with her as well. It takes more effort at times, but I practice setting my agenda aside to really listen to her needs.

The path has not been even, straight, or fearless. It has been uneven and rocky, and I have stumbled more than once. More than once I have been ready to hightail it and run. The cave has looked very tempting because I know I might feel a semblance of control there. But each time I pull back a little less and create an opportunity to learn more about myself and this relationship, I learn more about the true value and nature of commitment.

Let's now move forward together in a new direction: preparing him, you, and me for meaningful commitment.

EIGHT

COMMITMENT ISN'T ON THE SALES RACK

We all know that growing is not a thing of effort, but is the result of an inward life principle of growth...the wonderful divine life of an indwelling Holy Ghost.

HANNAH WHITALL SMITH

In order for change to occur, you must first become what you expect from others.

This seems to be a simple enough truth—that you must have the very qualities you seek from others. Even though I'm not usually equipped to handle this notion, I must admit that it is true. If you want peace, you must be peaceful. If you want love, you must be loving. If you want commitment, you must be capable of commitment yourself. But putting this into practice is quite another thing, and we all need to understand that doing so is part of the price we pay for commitment.

Dietrich Bonhoeffer understood the cost of commitment. He was a passionate and charismatic young man, blond-haired and blue-eyed, a pacifist during the Nazi regime. Bold and brave, he was willing to take a stand while others marched in lockstep behind a terrifying leader. Being a German who opposed Hitler during World War II was a life-threatening proposition. Asked why he took action, Bonhoeffer said he could not stand by and watch this madman wreak havoc on innocent bystanders. He had to do his best to avert disaster.

Bonhoeffer chose to be an advocate for Jews and helped a group escape to Switzerland, which led to his arrest and imprisonment in 1943. In fact, Bonhoeffer was one of a handful of Christians who actively opposed national socialism. His path of commitment led to his death. He was hanged in the concentration camp at Flossenburg on April 9, 1945—the same month Hitler committed suicide.

But this revolutionary Christian who opposed an egocentric monster also had a softer side. He was committed to a woman whom he loved. Listen to part of one love letter—hidden away in the archives of history until recently: "Wait with me, I beg you! Let me embrace you long and tenderly, let me kiss you and love you and stroke the sorrow from your brow." These words are not from a character in a sultry Harlequin romance. They are the words of the impassioned champion of radical discipleship to his fiancée, Maria von Wedemeyer.

Wendy Murray Zoba, in an article for *Christianity Today* titled "CT Classic: Bonhoeffer in Love," says this of Bonhoeffer's passionate letters:

> These sentiments—and more like them—written during his imprisonment from 1942 to 1945 present a new aspect of Bonhoeffer, showing him to be surprisingly amorous, but in a way altogether consistent with his theology of *costly grace*. Such love for Maria was "costly" because Bonhoeffer was forced to relinquish

it; it was "grace," because after 37 years of heady bachelorhood, he tasted of the wellspring of romantic possibility.[1]

We might easily idolize Bonhoeffer. I have admired him for years as a martyr for his Christian faith and for standing up to Adolph Hitler at a time when bowing down might have saved his life. To know that he had a love that would never see its full promise simply heightens the poignancy of his life. Zoba continues:

> He loved her, longed for her, and she for him. And the tenderness and optimism behind this collection of letters is what drives the book. The reader languishes with them as week after week, unto months, unto years, the couple anticipates the time when they will sit together on the couch at the Patzig (Maria's family estate) and hold hands.

But this would never happen.

Dietrich Bonhoeffer's story is more dramatic than our own. Yet in his life of passion and devotion to one God and one woman, we see a singularity of purpose and commitment that we can respect and attempt to emulate. This is precisely what so many of us are seeking—one man, one woman, in complete commitment to each other and to God.

Avoiding Paying the Price

Bonhoeffer is a tough act to follow. Here was a man of emotional and spiritual integrity who was willing to pay the ultimate price of commitment. Too often, the rest of us are far more frugal with our giving. Perhaps we are too caught up in the everyday battles life sends our way. We must deal with divorce, remarriage, blended families, hostility, addictions, and any number of other issues. We struggle in our marriages and our relationships and our careers. Our love letters are probably packed away, dusty for lack of use. We falter in the face of emotional and spiritual commitment.

In *Ten Stupid Things Women Do to Mess Up Their Lives,* Dr. Laura Schlessinger effectively lays out the ingenious ways women (and men) find to avoid paying the price of commitment. She has a chapter in her book titled "Stupid Forgiving: I Know He's Adulterous, Addicted, Controlling, Insensitive, and Violent...but Other Than That..."[2] Hmmm. Schlessinger starts the chapter with some attention-getting hyperbole:

> Have you ever noticed how motionless a praying mantis remains, no matter what is going on around it? The only creature capable of equaling that limitless patience and tolerance is the human female—who will invent millions of excuses to avoid getting out of the way of an oncoming bad relationship or permanently escaping from one in which she's already ensconced.

Dr. Laura cites several themes regarding the cost of commitment that are worthy of our consideration.

Being Dishonest with Yourself

Recently I counseled a 45-year-old woman named Anita, who wanted help with her marriage. She explained that her husband was distant, controlling, argumentative, and angry. She walked on pins and needles around him in order to avoid conflict. She wanted me to tell her how to talk to him so that he might take a more active interest in their marriage.

We spent several sessions discussing things she had tried and the impact they had had on their marriage. For every effort she made, her husband, Tom, seemed to have a countermove. When she tried to get close, he moved away. When she asked to talk, he said he would do it later. For the most part, nothing seemed to work. He seemed to have little invested in their marriage though according to Anita both were committed Christians and not seeking new relationships or an end to their own.

Near the end of our fourth counseling session, Anita offered another piece of information she thought might be helpful.

"There is probably something else I should tell you," she said.

"What's that?" I asked.

"He smokes marijuana. He has been using for our whole marriage. I don't know if it makes any difference in regard to what we're talking about, but I thought I should tell you."

I paused, incredulous.

"Anita, why didn't you mention it earlier?"

"Well, it's kind of embarrassing for a 40-something woman to be with a dope smoker, don't you think? I always assumed he would give it up when I did, 20 years ago. But he hasn't. I hate it, but he says he uses it for recreational purposes only. Maybe he's right."

"Do you believe that? Do you believe it's merely recreational?"

She looked down at her hands and sighed.

"No, not really. But there is no use arguing with him, and I don't know if it really affects our relationship. He does seem tired all the time, but says it has nothing to do with the marijuana. He also seems more irritable if he doesn't use anything for a while."

"Anita," I said softly. "Drug use affects every relationship. Drug use affects every personality. Certainly it affects how he interacts with you."

Anita was a classic example of someone who was not being honest with herself. She had been in denial for years, unwilling to face the real cost of commitment, which always begins with honesty. We cannot create a healthy, committed relationship when that relationship is rife with deception, addiction, and blatant neglect.

In the following weeks, I encouraged Anita to research marijuana use, how it affects the personality of the user, and how it impacts marriages. I also asked her to think about her behaviors and how they were enabling Tom to maintain his addiction.

She had her work cut out for her, but the first step was honesty. And that meant being honest with herself and then being honest with Tom.

Resisting Change

You may rail against your partner's unwillingness to change, but you also need to look in your own corner to see if that same trait applies to you. Are you willing to face things honestly? Are you willing to make changes in how you approach him? Are you willing to demand emotional and physical commitment in your relationship, or are you willing to let him go his own way with little regard for you or your marriage?

My practice is filled with people who want relief but don't want to change. Think about it. We want instant solutions, miracle cures, a genie in a bottle. When it comes to weight loss, most want quick-fix diets, pills, or fast surgical procedures to look better. The same is true with emotional and relational problems. Clients are always disappointed to learn that my magic wand is broken. In fact, I never had a magic wand at all. The best I can offer is a willingness to walk alongside as we search for solutions together.

Expect genuine commitment to involve significant change and considerable cost. You will need to determine whether you and your mate are ready and willing to participate completely in your relationship. If not, your chances of success are very small.

Complaining About Your Choices

I have often considered placing a sign outside the door of my office that says No Victims Allowed. I have not done so but only for fear of losing business and having to resort to my old job of washing dishes at Denny's.

Folks who come to me for counseling quickly learn that playing the victim is unhealthy. Yes, sometimes life bites us. But more often, we bite ourselves. A thorough analysis of our lives often reveals embarrassing examples of our continued habit of creating problems for which we would prefer not to take responsibility.

Anita discovered that she had chosen her husband because she liked his daredevil attitude. She had falsely believed he would grow out of his addictive personality and behavior patterns, and now she was surprised at how much they bothered her.

But why was she surprised? He had used marijuana throughout their marriage. Why was she annoyed now? Why not 20 years ago? I'm not blaming Anita for being angry. I can certainly empathize with her and her circumstances. But she was fully aware of them before she entered into the relationship. She now had to acknowledge her past decisions and consider her future options from a mature perspective.

Schlessinger says, "There are times when such trade-offs—staying in a not-so-good situation for reasons—will be your choice. The point is that you need to make the choice consciously and maturely. If you don't, you leave yourself open to disappointment, frustration, anger and hurt."[3] I would add that in addition to making decisions consciously and responsibly, we must make them prayerfully. God is bigger than any foolish choices we may have made 20 years ago.

Not Choosing, or Practicing the Art of Avoidance

Now we step on a few toes—including mine. The delicate art of procrastination is something I have practiced for decades. If there is a way for me not to make a decision about a critical issue, I can usually find it.

I remember a difficult discussion I needed to have with Christie concerning our path of commitment to one another. The situation was complicated because I feared hurting her feelings or offending her. Although I knew and had written about the practice of "speaking the truth in love," practicing what I preached was a real challenge. It is much easier for me to tell others how to address a thorny issue than to risk getting pricked myself.

Early in our relationship, I was unclear where she stood spiritually. I was attracted to her and fond of her but was unsure how committed she was to practicing a Christian lifestyle. Specifically, I wanted us to attend church every Sunday and knew that was not part of her recent pattern.

But how was I going to bring up something as delicate as one's spiritual life? Who was I to tell her how to live her life? What if she found me to be a self-righteous, pontificating egotist? Worse, what if she found me to be hypocritical—wanting increased spirituality in our relationship when I didn't always act like a good Christian myself? What if she noticed and commented on my inconsistent participation in church activities?

Well, I initially dealt with this the way many of us would—by avoiding it. I found myself hinting about my desire to attend church regularly. I told Christie how much I enjoyed attending church with her. I praised the pastor, sang the praises of the choir, and danced around the topic quite remarkably for months. All the while, I knew my avoidance would not work for us in the long run. True commitment would cost me courage and honesty. I couldn't hide.

Interestingly, each time I hinted at my concern, Christie responded favorably. She always agreed about the importance of attending church regularly. She purchased a Bible study program for us to work through together. She liked the pastor. Still, I stopped short of saying it—"I need to know whether you are committed to regular church attendance and making our spiritual life an important part of our daily life."

I finally had "the talk" with her, and as I suspected, she responded favorably. Real commitment involves knowing what you know and acting accordingly.

Living Without Integrity

The word *integrity* comes from the Latin word *integer,* which means wholeness or completeness. When we live with integrity we live wholly. We act in a way that is consistent with our beliefs. To do so, we obviously must know what we believe and why we believe it. That is why I encourage all of my clients to journal—to practice writing out their thoughts, feelings, and desires.

The act of dumping painful feelings onto the page frees us from carrying the burden in our minds. Like prayer, it is a way to pour out our aching souls to our heavenly Father. Something about it is liberating.

I also recommend journaling because I want people to experience integrity—wholeness. I want them to know the feeling of understanding what they feel, why they feel it, and what they can do about it in a way that is consistent with their nature.

Nearly everyone I counsel is, in some way, acting in a manner that is inconsistent with their nature. They are betraying themselves. They believe one thing but act in a way that opposes that belief. They say they are fine when they are seething inside. They say they cannot think of any way to change when they know precisely what they need to do differently. They feel painful emotions but do everything in their power to stuff them away—out of sight, out of mind.

When we practice journaling or praying about what is true for us, we see what we need to be happy. We can no longer hide behind illusions masquerading as truth. "The truth will set you free" is not just a nice line from Scripture—it is the truth. Prayerful journaling will help you recognize the truth and make healthier choices about what you need to do to be whole and complete. It is a positive first step to living with integrity.

"Something's Wrong with Me" and Other Self-Doubts

To live with integrity is risky business. Most of us remain content not knowing what we really think, not doing what we really want to do, not deciding what is really best for us. Living this way may be easier than living with convictions and action, but it is immeasurably less fulfilling. We would do well to stop living in worlds clouded by self-doubt.

Many people wonder what is best for them. You may be in that place. You may live in a world of confusion, uncertain about whether your man is right for you. Uncertain about whether to push him harder and demand more or to simply settle for the way things are. Living with this lack of clarity can be very difficult. It can also be a rut, a place of unhappiness that you decorate and settle into for the long haul.

I often pray for clarity in my life, but I know at times I have my fingers crossed behind my back. I know the bright lights of clarity will cost me. True clarity will force me to act on my convictions.

Working your way to a committed relationship demands that you move away from self-doubt and begin to trust what you believe to be true. If your thoughts are bathed in prayer and you are soaking up the Word of God, you must trust your gut. Avoiding decisions because of self-doubt can become a bad habit that will keep you stuck in a life without fulfillment.

Committed to Pain, or "This Is All I Deserve"

You may believe you are willing to pay the price of commitment when in fact you are selling yourself short. You may have set the bar so low that both your mate and you believe you have a healthy, committed relationship even though that is not the case at all.

Because of frustration and discouragement, many women I've worked with set their standards very low and then wonder why they feel anemic and despairing. Their thinking has become clouded. They believe that if their man calls once a week or offers tiny morsels of affection, they are getting all they deserve.

Beware of low expectations. They will seem to comfort you in the short run, but they will leave you resentful and angry over the long haul. Reflect earnestly on your self-image. Ask yourself the following questions:

- Do I deserve to be loved and cherished?
- Would anything in my past lead me to settle for less than that?
- Do I look around, see myself in the same boat as others, and tell myself that things aren't so bad?
- Have I always settled for less than I wanted?
- Am I settling for less now?

Polygamy Revisited

A number of women have told me that they were in relationships with men who wanted to see them and someone else simultaneously. Perhaps your man wants to maintain an open relationship. He says he is committed to you but wants to keep his options open. He tells you that you are special to him, but he is not ready to settle down. He offers this and a dozen other reasons to explain why the relationship must have limits—for the time being. You tell yourself that if you wait and remain willing to be one of several, things will work out.

A muted form of polygamy, both in and out of marriage, seems to be fashionable today. Your boyfriend has told you how much he cares for you. But he prefers an open relationship. Or perhaps we are talking about your husband, who has the audacity to expect you to understand when he "steps out" occasionally. It doesn't mean anything, he says. Not long ago, Patricia came to see me about this very issue.

A 38-year-old chemist with steel blue eyes and a sharp voice, she worked for the government, conducting research on disease processes. She came to see me because she was conflicted about her boyfriend of two years. He had recently announced that he wanted to spend weekends with another woman. He said he cared for both of them and wanted to explore the two possibilities. Her fantasies of a monogamous relationship were dashed now that she knew her boyfriend was fooling around. She obviously was worried about whether the relationship had a future.

We discussed the implications of tolerating her boyfriend's behavior, even temporarily while he decides: If he fools around and she stays, he learns that he doesn't have to do much to keep her. He learns that she does not seem to think that much of herself. And this is a further insult to her self-respect.

Clearly Patricia had little to gain and a lot to lose from this arrangement. This man made no clear promises to her, and she would only suffer if she frittered away her life on someone who would not commit. She chose wisely to let her two-timing boyfriend go.

Pursuing the Impossible Dream

If you have been to a success symposium lately or watched an Oprah special, you've heard that your potential is unlimited. You've heard that you can have whatever you set your sights on, that you should see endless possibilities, think expansively, and pursue impossible dreams. The words are sometimes so tantalizing that we lose our balance and perspective. At face value, the notion is so wonderful. Who doesn't want to believe in something like that? Who doesn't want to "beat the unbeatable foe"?

But wait! Does this language apply to blind, syrupy love and the commitment-phobic man who often accompanies it? No.

Is pressing on toward a foolish goal a wise thing to do? No.

The cost of commitment should not be confused with imprudent, wishful thinking. Although we may want to believe in the dream because it can soothe our wounded feelings, it is merely a Band-Aid. The pain returns when this counterfeit cure fails to heal the wound. Believing in something that simply is not true—hoping that he will commit when the odds scream against it—is nothing more than snake oil treatment. We want to believe the back label that says it will cure everything from boils to broken hearts, but the cost is high and the returns are sparse.

The Scriptures repeatedly advise us to be wise, to be prayerful, and to make good choices. Consider the words of the apostle John near the end of his life:

> God is light; in him there is no darkness at all. If we claim to have fellowship with him yet walk in the darkness, we lie and do not live by the truth. But if we walk in the light, as he is in the light, we have fellowship with one another, and the blood of Jesus, his Son, purifies us from all sin (1 John 1:5-7).

Walking in the light means allowing ourselves to see things as God sees them—and this inevitably means seeing trouble where trouble exists. Pursuing impossible dreams is actually another way to avoid paying the price of commitment.

Zacchaeus

The scene is the hot, dusty town of Jericho, where we find Jesus passing through. He had no initial intention of staying in Jericho, but God had made a divine appointment for Him. Luke, the physician, tells the story (Luke 19).

A wealthy, ill-reputed tax collector named Zacchaeus had heard the Galilean was entering Jericho, and he wanted to see who Jesus was. Like you and me, Zacchaeus was curious. Jesus' reputation had apparently crept into Zacchaeus' world, and so he wanted to check Him out.

But Zacchaeus had a problem. He was a short man and could not see Jesus because of the crowd. He had power and wealth, but I suspect that Zacchaeus was short on peacefulness in his life. Why else would he want to see Jesus? Why else would the story unfold the way it does? But I am getting ahead of myself.

Zacchaeus wants to connect with Jesus. But his wealth, power, and deceit are like pickets creating a fence between himself and

Christ. So Zacchaeus climbed up into a sycamore tree. Now here was an interesting sight. The rich, influential Zacchaeus climbing a tree to see the simple, gentle Jesus. Zacchaeus wants to see Jesus. But what he doesn't know is that Jesus wants to see him.

Then we have the divine appointment, similar to the ones you and I have had. Opportunities to step out of our daily grind to seek and find the Savior. Times when our hearts have been softened by the Spirit so that we can *really* see Jesus. And when we are ready, we will see Him and He will see us.

Jesus, of course, anticipated the encounter. He passed by where Zacchaeus was perched in the sycamore tree and spoke directly to him.

"Zacchaeus, come down immediately. I must stay at your house today." So Zacchaeus came down at once and welcomed Him gladly.

The people watching this encounter were aghast. They murmured at the spectacle of the righteous rabbi inviting Himself to the home of Zacchaeus, a known sinner. But then Jesus was always, is always, doing something unexpected. He changes hearts that are willing to be changed. Zacchaeus had obviously been preparing for a change. The story goes on to say that he paid back fourfold anyone he had cheated.

This is a wonderful tale that is easy to overlook because of its brevity. But it is worth our consideration when we discuss the cost of commitment. We not only catch a glimpse of Zacchaeus' willingness to pay the price of commitment by stepping out publicly and claiming allegiance to Jesus, we see Jesus' commitment too. He commits Himself publicly to Zacchaeus as well and invites Himself into the sinner's life—just as He invites Himself into our lives.

Jesus could easily have passed by Zacchaeus. He could have focused on getting to where He was going, just as you and I do on a busy day. He could have been taken up with the tyranny of the urgent, but He wasn't. Rank, power, image—these things have no meaning to Jesus. Zacchaeus discovered that they had no meaning for him either.

Imagine the relief Zacchaeus felt when he was given the opportunity to make things right. No demands, just opportunity. No pressure, just one person making a commitment to another.

Paying the Price for Commitment

Perhaps we are all a bit like Zacchaeus. We have been tentative, shortsighted. We have desired the expensive gift of commitment, but we have been shopping for it on the sales rack. Even though we want all the benefits of the real thing, we have been unwilling to pay the price, or perhaps we have been unwilling to demand it from our mate. It is now time to ready yourself to pay in full and to ask your man to pay this price as well. True commitment does not come cheap.

Let's consider what true commitment will cost. As you examine this list, please review and discuss it with the man in your life.

1. *Commitment demands dedication to each other's welfare and happiness.* Yes, it's true. Once we are in a serious, committed relationship, we must be conscious not only of what makes us happy but also what makes our mate happy. We must give up our self-centeredness. We must move beyond childish self-absorption and into other-relatedness. If we truly want our mate to be happy, we will dedicate ourselves to that end. We will reflect on those things we know bring him or her pleasure and then pursue them. Incidentally, we know that making our mate happy will bring happiness back to us as well. Mark Twain humorously illustrates this point in a story about a man and his wife:

> I woke up, with that smothered and unlocateable cry of "Mortimer! Mortimer!" wailing in my ears, and as soon as I could scrape my faculties together I reached over in the dark and then said:

"Evangeline, is that you calling? What is the matter? Where are you?"

"Shut up in the boot-closet. You ought to be ashamed to lie there and sleep on, and such an awful storm going on."

"Why, how can one be ashamed when he is asleep? It is unreasonable; a man can't be ashamed when he is asleep, Evangeline."

"You never try, Mortimer—you know very well you never try."

I caught the sounds of muffled sobs.

That sound smote dead the sharp speech that was on my lips, and I changed to—"I'm sorry, dear—I'm truly sorry. I never meant to act so."[4]

2. *Commitment demands responsibility to one another.* Committed relationships require that we take some measure of responsibility for our mates as well as for ourselves. We watch out for their welfare. We encourage them to take care of themselves because they are now a part of us. We want the best for them and let them know it.

3. *Commitment demands tolerance for life's inevitable storms.* Committed relating means that we are prepared for the challenges that come with closeness. We know and accept that times of conflict will inevitably come, but they will not distance us from one another. We might disagree, but the fabric of our relationship is strong and can weather these difficult times. Whether these are challenges to our health, finances, or emotions, we are prepared to pay the cost and stick it out together.

4. *Commitment demands that we let go of reservations.* I have already mentioned that commitment means that we lock the back door. We leave ourselves no outs—short of serious issues such as violence, infidelity, or abandonment. When conflict inevitably

rears its head, we don't consider leaving the relationship. Instead, we think creatively about how this problem can be solved.

5. *Commitment demands that we let go of independence.* Committed relating means we are no longer free to do our own thing. Earlier in our lives, that was possible, but once we make a true commitment, we must consider everything we do in context of the relationship. This is not a bad thing. Interdependence is liberating and exciting.

6. *Commitment demands fidelity.* Nothing tears at the fabric of a marriage or relationship like unfaithfulness. During my years as a counselor, I have seen no issue as corrosive to the life of a marriage as infidelity. Posturing never works. Committed couples must eradicate infidelity from their relationships. Faithfulness is an absolute necessity for healthy relating.

7. *Commitment demands emotional transparency and emotional vulnerability.* As I have stated previously, you and your mate must be committed to one another physically *and* emotionally. You must be dedicated to learning more about each other every day. You must be committed to sharing more of yourselves. And that means giving up superficiality. The height of love is to truly understand one another and to be understood.

As you review this list, you will quickly see that Jesus exemplifies these behaviors. He is fully committed to us without reservation, and He wants our fidelity to Him. He is transparent, willing for us to know Him and wanting to fully know us.

An objective examination of these items will also go a long way to help determine whether you are in a healthy, committed relationship. This is a perfect opportunity to improve your relationship by assessing where you and your mate need to make adjustments.

Reinforcing the Foundation

We dare not build the house of marriage on the sands of emotion or passion. Although we certainly wish those feelings would remain strong forever, this is often not the case. The passion that drew you to your mate may fluctuate at times, but this need not weaken the stability of your relationship if it is based on true commitment. Dr. Aaron Beck, author of *Love Is Never Enough*, makes this clear:

> Love alone is not enough to provide the connective tissue of a relationship. The other basic qualities that strengthen the marital bond and ensure the durability of a relationship arise gradually and spontaneously... Once developed, the forces for stability—commitment, loyalty, trust—protect the closeness, intimacy, and security of the loving bond. Knowing that your mate will never desert you, for instance, gives you a sense of security and confidence in the relationship.[5]

All of us long to feel secure in our relationships. We want to know that our mate will *never* leave. We want stability, loyalty, commitment. Without these things we cannot feel safe—our house cannot stand.

Commitment does not come cheap. It will cost you and your mate dearly. But it is worth the price—the full price!

NINE

When the Princess Is Ready, the Prince Will Appear

Men and women of integrity and simplicity of heart, loving to follow righteousness, are by the secret touches of a holy Light guided by God.

ROBERT BARCLAY

Once upon a time, long ago, there lived a girl who was sweet and kind, patient and cute. She was the opposite in all ways from her stepmother, who was mean, angry, and ugly. The stepmother was jealous of the girl and put her to work doing all kinds of disgusting tasks. The stepmother's two daughters also despised this girl because of her beauty and pleasing demeanor. And so this lovely girl was made to sleep among the ashes in the chimney corner, which is how she became known as a cinder wench, or as we have come to know her, Cinderella.

One day, the king and his wife hosted a ball for their unmarried son and invited all the eligible maidens in the kingdom to attend. The king hoped that the prince would choose a bride. When the invitation arrived at Cinderella's house, all three girls were excited. But Cinderella's excitement was quickly doused by her stepsisters' taunting.

"You can't go," they said with disdain. "You have nothing fit to wear, and you live amongst the cinders."

The evening of the ball arrived, and the stepsisters paraded around in their finery, taking great delight in rubbing salt in Cinderella's wounds. They flounced into their coach and off to the ball, leaving Cinderella behind, her spirits shattered.

Enter one fairy godmother. The godmother quickly assessed the situation—Cinderella wanted to go to the ball in the worst way but had no clothing appropriate for such an event and no means of getting there.

But we know that in fairy tales, magic can take place with the wave of a wand. A pumpkin became a gilded carriage, six mice became dappled-gray stallions for the coach, a fat rat was turned into a jolly coachman, and two lizards appeared as footmen. A few more waves of the wand transformed Cinderella into a beautifully dressed woman in a shimmering gown, her feet adorned in delicate glass slippers. She was now ready to proceed to the ball.

At the ball, the prince was ready to find the princess he had dreamed of. Perhaps, we might surmise, he was ready to meet a good person—a kind and wonderful person.

But remember, Cinderella had to watch the clock because her fairy godmother had been careful to warn her that the magic would end at midnight. Indeed, at the stroke of twelve, realizing that she was about to be transformed back into a cinder wench, she ran from the ball with the prince chasing after her. She dropped one glass slipper, the only clue to her identity. The prince was dejected and set out to find the owner of the slipper.

He tried the slipper on all of the maidens, but it would not fit. Finally, Cinderella offered her foot for the fitting while her sisters scoffed at the absurd notion that she could be the future princess. Not only did the slipper fit, but Cinderella pulled out the matching slipper, casting off any doubts that she had been the woman who had won the prince's heart.

At that moment, the fairy godmother waved her wand again and Cinderella was dressed in her beautiful gown once more. Adorned as a princess, more beautiful and charming than ever, she married her prince a few days later. Instead of seeking revenge against her stepsisters, she forgave them and offered them a place in her court.

Don't you just love a good fairy tale? And what if this fairy tale could be your own one day? What a nice story that would be.

But this is just a fairy tale, right? Certainly, this could never happen in real life, you say.

Not so quick. There are some important considerations for us in this tale.

Cinderella is a good person. We read that in addition to her outer beauty, she had a good heart. Certainly this was immediately apparent to the prince. She had taken a lifetime to ready herself for the opportunity at the ball. Each of us is in the same situation—those times when preparation meets opportunity—what some commonly refer to as luck. I think it has more to do with building character.

Cinderella's story reminds me of the biblical account of Joseph. You may recall that this handsome boy, his father's favorite, has character as well. His strength of character shines through as the story unfolds. He is ridiculed by his older brothers (certainly a potential character-building situation), and out of fierce jealousy they plot to end his life. They throw him into a pit and leave him for dead. (More character building.) But God has other plans. Through a series of twists and turns, challenges and opportunities for Joseph to either rise to a higher calling or sully himself in improper conduct, the young man makes positive choices and ultimately becomes a high-ranking official in Pharaoh's court.

What is remarkable about this story is Joseph's response to the many calamities that befall him. The details of his life suggest that each event that could have ruined him actually prepared him for greatness. He had every right to hate his brothers. He had every right to be vindictive. But he is far too classy to get caught up in bitterness and resentment. In the end, he forgives his brothers for trying to kill him.

Joseph is good, but he is far more than that. He has faith. He can see the bigger picture. Listen to his insight: "And now, do not be distressed and do not be angry with yourselves for selling me here, because it was to save lives that God sent me ahead of you...So then, it was not you who sent me here, but God" (Genesis 45:5,8). Instead of poverty and famine, he offers his father and brothers the riches Pharaoh provides because of Joseph's favored position.

Goodness pays off. Right prevails. Faith and character create opportunity. Years of preparation yield great rewards.

The bottom line is this: When the princess is ready, the prince will appear. You will be prepared when the opportunity presents itself, and it will.

Getting Ready for Your Prince

You may initially scoff at my suggestion that if you make the proper preparations, your prince will come. "It's just a fairy tale, Dr. Hawkins," you might say. "These kinds of things don't happen in real life."

Well, allow me to make a bold assertion: If you make the proper preparations, you can find a man who will commit himself to you emotionally, physically, and spiritually. In fact, this is our next stage of commitment: preparing for your prince. With the right preparation, you can have a committed, healthy relationship.

It is all possible and available to you. But first you must deal effectively and realistically with the preparations.

I understand that the story of Cinderella is just that—a story. That does not mean, however, that we cannot learn from it. It does not mean that we cannot use our imagination to find principles that will help our situation, or glean strength from Cinderella's tenacity and resourcefulness. Let's consider again her plight.

Imagine Cinderella's discouragement as she faced this monumental task. She had to find a way to weave her rags into a beautiful evening gown, change her pumpkin into a gold, gilded coach, and transform her mice into majestic stallions. (Yes, she had a little help in this endeavor.) You too must identify and change those things that could hinder you from having a committed relationship. You must find a way to convert your weaknesses into strengths, your failures into successes, your challenges into opportunities.

Any rats, rags, or stray mice lying around?

Let's look together at some of the preparations you must make. And by the way, you too have a fairy godmother—the Holy Spirit—who will help you make the necessary alterations.

Preparing Your Attitude

What attitude do you need to become a princess? It is one that always keeps an eye on possibility. It is one of hopefulness. You *must* have the conviction that you deserve a prince of a man.

This may be obvious to you, but I am surprised by the number of women who talk about wanting to date or marry a wonderful man but feel too inadequate to find one. I am amazed at how often I hear this statement: "I just don't know how or where I could possibly find a good man." I ask women to really think about it and then come up with some ideas about where princely men might be spending time. Many remain baffled by the question, although a few are able to come up with an idea or two.

Let's talk about where you are most likely to find a good man if you are single. Let's also talk about where you are least likely to find a good man.

Bad locations: a tavern, a local dance club that serves as a "meat market," your front door.

Good locations: your church singles group, a Christian dating organization, your place of employment, your volunteer experiences.

You must believe that you can find a good man, that you deserve a good man, and that you can attract a good man. You must make yourself available and take the risks necessary to attract your prince. If you are not at that point yet, don't despair. You simply have some work to do.

What should your attitude be if you are married?

The same.

You are still Cinderella, preparing yourself for your prince. You must believe that you are a princess, a bride of Christ whom others must treat with honor.

When you believe that about yourself, your attitude will come across in the way you act and the way you expect your man to treat you. It will also come through in the way you treat your man. Sometimes treating him like a prince can transform him into one!

Preparing Your Expectations

When you change your attitude, you change your expectations. You will want to convey to your man, in subtle and not so subtle terms, that you deserve to be treated with respect and dignity, and that you will settle for nothing less than a relationship filled with intimacy. You deserve a man who will work on the relationship with you, who will strive to deepen his emotional and spiritual life, and who will commit himself to you completely and faithfully.

The apostle Paul has many things to say about expectations in marriage—and in committed relationships.

> Submit to one another out of reverence for Christ. Wives, submit to your husbands as to the Lord...Husbands, love your wives, just as Christ loved the church and gave himself up for her to make her holy, cleansing her by the washing with water through the word, and to present her to himself as a radiant church, without stain or wrinkle or any other blemish, but holy and blameless. In this same way, husbands ought to love their wives as their own bodies (Ephesians 5:21-28).

I have stated previously that I think women ought not lower the bar for men, but in fact, raise it. Too many women settle for too little from their men. And that may be true for you today. If it is, consider raising the bar. Consider expecting more from your man. If you are truly to be happy, you must have a relationship that is filled with zest, emotional warmth, spiritual integrity, and yes, commitment. If you don't have it now, you need to start looking for ways to attain it.

Preparing Your Presentation

When you get ready to ask for more, your presentation will be critical. A princess is not overly demanding, arrogant, or critical. She is elegant and classy. She has a way of insisting on what she needs and being clear when expressing her needs and desires.

I know a woman who, despite her offbeat, spiked hair, has perfected an elegant presentation. Katherine is a modern woman in her fifties. She is now the wife of a wonderful minister.

But many years ago, I watched Katherine, who had been married before, grapple with the painful aspects of her divorce. She suffered as people within the church said hurtful things about her. She once shared in a small group that she felt unfairly judged by others who did not know the details of her failed marriage.

But Katherine always carried herself with dignity. She survived the divorce and gradually moved into dating. She eventually married a minister who had been widowed, and they now enjoy a bountiful marriage. Her divorce did not stop him from falling in love with and marrying her.

What is so special about Katherine? She has a rare presence that is quite noticeable. She has an air of confidence and a bold, spiritual depth. She knows her Bible and isn't afraid to share her thoughts and insights about it. More importantly, Katherine is authentic and genuine and knows she is loved by God. This inner confidence projects into an outer radiance that makes all things possible for her.

Preparing Your Vision

When your attitude is right and you have developed a clear set of expectations, you will also need to have a firm vision. A firm vision is a picture you carry in your mind of the outcome you want. This vision is specific—it might sound like the description I heard from a client named Joan. "I want a Christian man who is loving, tender, and kind. He needs to be athletic, to love children, and to be interested in travel. He needs to be compassionate and have a heart for the hurting and less fortunate in the world."

Susan was a 35-year-old married woman who recently came to see me because she was dissatisfied with her husband and their marriage. She sat primly in the chair, toying with her pearl necklace. When asked what was wrong in her marriage, she was unable to clearly describe what was troubling her. She fumbled with her words, and we eventually agreed that if she could not state what she wanted, her husband would naturally be confused. We worked together for several weeks before she was able to articulate this:

> I want my husband to date me. I want to go out at least once a week on some special outing, and I want him to treat me special. I want him to send me flowers once

in a while, remember my birthday and other special occasions, and take me away once every few months on some exciting adventure.

Studies show that the more clearly and precisely you are able to describe your vision, the more likely you are to achieve it. Rehearse where you want to live, the kind of house you want to live in, and the kind of man you want to occupy it with you. Prayerfully share with the Lord the dreams you have, and let Him help you with the rest.

Preparing Your Heart

During the darkest days of my separation and divorce, my mother and father were my stalwart companions. When I was uncertain about how to proceed, they reminded me that if I simply put one foot in front of the other, I was sure to make progress. My mother repeatedly offered me these encouraging words from the prophet Jeremiah. Perhaps they will be helpful to you.

> "For I know the plans I have for you," declares the LORD, "plans to prosper you and not to harm you, plans to give you hope and a future. Then you will call upon me and come and pray to me, and I will listen to you. You will seek me and find me when you seek me with all your heart" (Jeremiah 29:11).

These words were lifesavers for me. Although they were written long ago for other people, they come from the same God who loves me and has a vision and purpose for my life. They come from the heart of God, a heart that longs for my heart to be whole and healed. A heart that reminds me that I have a bright future.

The psalmist says, "Create in me a clean heart, O God; and renew a right spirit within me" (Psalm 51:10 KJV). Little is more important to bring to your relationship than a clean heart, one that is free of false motives, that is sensitive to God's heart, that is willing to be broken for the sake of Christ.

Have you asked God for wisdom about your current relationship? Are you sure the man you're considering marrying is right for you? Are you sure you are being the best woman you can be for him, and for Him? Remember, before you can ask for something, you must first be willing and able to give it yourself.

I could say that simple luck brought Christie to me after my divorce. Or I could say that God determined the right time. I choose to consider yet another possibility. I think it was the right time because I had done some personal work *and* because God was involved in our meeting.

I met Christie under an unusual set of circumstances. She saw me at a professional gathering and initiated the contact. Introducing herself to me was a bold and extraordinary move on her part. I am certainly glad that she took that initiative. Our meeting occurred long after Christie had been divorced and two years after my divorce was final. By then, I had done a great deal of personal therapy and recovery from my breakup.

I had dated a lot the year before we met. It was a rich time of learning about myself, about what kind of life I wanted and what things I needed to work on in my emotional and spiritual life. I had been through a few short-term relationships in which I learned more about myself and the changes I needed to make in my personality. I learned that I wanted to be with someone with integrity, someone who was free from "excess baggage" and truly available for a relationship. (Not all are, you know!)

During that time, I thoughtfully considered what I wanted in a woman and set out in search of someone with those qualities. Initially, I believed I wanted someone rich and powerful, but I soon discovered that I did not want that at all. These were shallow and empty qualities, of little value in a relationship. They often seemed to fit those who had little spiritual depth, something extremely important to me. I ultimately decided I wanted someone who was sensitive, bright, and ready to create both a home and a rich relationship. I definitely did not want to find a fellow workaholic.

I used the time after my divorce to deepen my spiritual life. I determined to only date women who had a deep spiritual commitment and who would share those aspirations with me. Christie met those requirements.

I prayed the following prayer with Christie recently: "Lord, please guide us to the right church. Please help us know what we need to do regarding our careers. Please guide us in the paths You would have us take."

Without waiting for me to stop, she simply added, "And help us to know when to be quiet and listen."

Her words surprised me. I had taken for granted that I would, of course, listen to any counsel offered by the Spirit. But I realized that was not necessarily true. I am good at offering up prayer upon prayer, request upon request. However, I am not nearly so good at being quiet and listening.

Are you really listening for the soft voice of God nudging you in a particular direction? If, like me, you will agree to stay quiet and take note, that voice will provide instruction.

Authenticity

Cinderella's marriage to the prince was not what made her a princess in the true sense of the word. Though a simple woman, Cinderella was a princess at heart from the beginning. The story illustrates that she had class and dignity long before hearing about the ball, long before knowing a prince was in her future. In her heart, Cinderella knew that she was a princess, and she acted accordingly.

Living authentically is an important issue. Too often we live confused, misdirected, misguided lives. We lack purpose, vision, and direction. Marsha Sinetar, author of the book *Ordinary People as Monks and Mystics*, says, "To find in ourselves what makes life worth living is risky business, for it means that once we know we must seek it. It also means that without it life will be value-less."[1] In the same vein, Christina Baldwin, in her wonderful book *Life's Companion: Journal Writing as a Spiritual Quest*, says, "Our primary task in life is to discover and define our life purpose and then to accomplish it to the best of our ability...The way we think about life and journey makes our dreams for the future real—a time and place we head for, as surely as we head for home."[2]

But what does this have to do with becoming a princess, you might ask? Simply this. The most direct and exciting path toward princess living is being clear about who you are and who God created you to be, and then living into it. The most attractive person is not the one with the most exquisite appearance, but the one with inner beauty and clarity. I found that when I refined my search, and was clear about it, I was able to make much better choices in my dating. Listen again to Baldwin's words:

> The future expands and contracts depending on what it is we are trying to think about. We start practicing very early for the lives we want to lead, the lives we think we are capable of leading, the lives we are told by family and society are appropriate and possible. Our earliest sense of capability develops out of this dreaming. We make space for ourselves in the wide open fields of the future. We begin to imagine who we might be and what our purpose is.[3]

Gina is a 50-year-old woman who is trying to become authentic. Known to me only through our long-distance phone conversations, Gina tells me that she is deeply discouraged with her husband, a recovering alcoholic who Gina says is both distant and angry.

After 20 years of arguing and seemingly endless conflict, she is trying to discover who she is. She has danced so long to this stifling music that she no longer feels any joy in life. She wonders what she might expect from her marriage and is equally discouraged by her own behavior—she finds herself barking back at her husband and treating him with similar disrespect.

Gina is profoundly discouraged and lost. She has few friends, lives solely to accommodate her demanding husband, and wants counsel on how to proceed with her life. She has much work to do, including rediscovering her personal identity and what is important to her. She long ago lost the dreams of her youth. She wonders if God has abandoned her. Her princess has been hidden away in the attic for many, many years.

As I listen to Gina, I must admit that I feel somewhat discouraged as well. Her task is daunting. She has lived long in the shadow of oppression. The marriage appears to offer little to salvage, but God is big, and He is part of this plan. At least she called me. She is angry and wants more from life. She is a Christian, and although her faith is faint, it is enough to work with. Gina, like you and me, has a problem. She must dig deep into herself and into her relationship with the Lord to find the beginnings of a solution. She will need to build on the strength she showed when she called me in the first place. She must find ways to consider who she is and what she needs from her husband. She must find new ways to communicate those needs to him and discover how she may be able to offer him some things in return. She has lost her princess qualities and will need to find ways to once again enrich her life. And she must realize that enrichment may be something she must find on her own.

Gina is in a difficult situation, one that you may keenly understand. She will need to do some reconstructive work and start rocking the boat. She needs to examine where she lost her genuine life, rediscover it, and then go after it again. Undoubtedly this will take significant work. We will explore how much her husband is willing to participate in this process with her. It may involve boundaries and perhaps confrontations. She will need to ready herself for these difficult times. This will take some archaeological work, but in the process she may become as excited as the

Egyptologist Howard Carter when he found the tomb of the boy-king, Tutankhamen. Like Carter, Gina may strike gold.

Steps Toward a Conscious Commitment

John Welwood, in his book *Journey of the Heart,* talks about transforming obstacles to commitment into opportunities. He says, "Commitment means choosing to work with those obstacles that interfere with the free flow of love, both in ourselves and our relationships."

Welwood outlines the steps that are necessary if you are genuine about establishing a true commitment with your mate. Ask yourself if you and your mate are ready to take the following steps.

1. *Making a Genuine Connection.*

> Just as the body of a guitar amplifies and enriches the vibration of the strings to produce a full, rich musical sound, similarly, the resonance between two beings amplifies and enriches the qualities of each...Out of this passionate resonance grows a devotion to each other's unfolding—which can allow them to preserve through difficult times and overcome any obstacles that threaten to come between them.[4]

2. *Testing the Connection: Working with Whatever Arises.* Welwood tells us that the "penetrating quality of an honest, loving connection wears away our facades, bringing out the best and the worst in us."[5] Isn't that the truth? All of our fears, insecurities, and resistances to intimacy come to the surface. Unfinished business from the past is suddenly laid bare, right there in the middle of our here-and-now relating. We need to see this as an opportunity to clear up past issues so that they do not cloud our current relationship. Although we may be tempted to blame our mate for our current difficulties, we should always double-check

and make sure the stuff that has arisen isn't old, unfinished business from our past.

3. *Forging a Container: Including All of Who We Are.* Welwood says that having a healthy commitment to one another creates a spacious container in which to deal with the material that may arise from our past as well as our present. It is a safe container where couples can look critically at the foibles they bring to the relationship—and everyone brings some. This container allows us to accommodate our mate's feelings, struggles, and complexities, and he or she is able to do the same for us. In this safe place, we look at the feelings that arise, listen to them, learn what they can teach us, and ultimately, accept them. Each partner agrees that this safe place will be free from shame, judgment, or ridicule. Instead, it will be a place of commitment where each person can grow and become all that God wants him or her to be. It is the place where you can grow into a princess, and he can grow into a prince.

After the Divorce

I was an emotional wreck during my marital separation and for a long time after the divorce. Many times I would pull the car to the side of the road and weep for my lost marriage. I called friends who encouraged me to share my pain and reminded me to eat and to drink lots of water. I sometimes shared more than usual with my clients simply because the emotion was so near the surface. I was healing and in process.

Although I tried to piece my life back together, I faltered in many ways. I sought professional counseling—the wounded healer seeking healing—and pursued God more earnestly. I wrapped myself in the blanket of my friends' affections and support. My fairy godmother, the Holy Spirit, provided many opportunities to be loved, cared for, and slowly healed. But healing took time.

I didn't know how broken I was until time passed and I was able to view things in retrospect. If you were to ask me how I was doing a year after my divorce, I would have told you I was getting along fairly well. In fact, I thought I was ready for a new relationship in my life. Boy, was I wrong. Attempts at relating were fraught with difficulties. I was about as ready for a princess as Jack Nicholson's character in *As Good as It Gets.* My warts were readily apparent to everyone but me. I was too needy. I was too emotional. I was too hungry for affection and love—not the best qualities to bring into a new relationship.

I am now several years beyond my divorce, and I am feeling human once again. Although I feel healthy, even now I have doubts about myself. I have mentioned how I continue to struggle with the very issues I am writing about in this book. I feel ready to commit myself to Christie six days out of seven—but every once in a while I wonder about my readiness. We are in the phase of "preparing ourselves for a committed relationship." I am trying to become a prince for my princess.

I have also gone through times of questioning my princess. I have asked Christie some very difficult questions:

- Will you love me forever?
- Will you always be faithful?
- Will you help me when I go through my predictable and unpredictable struggles?
- Will you allow me to help you?
- Will you share your most private feelings with me?
- Will you commit to enriching our spiritual life together?

Some of my questioning has certainly been made more acute and intense because of the rejection I carry from my failed marriage. Some of it is normal to anyone beginning a new relationship.

As a general rule, the more questions you ask at the start of the relationship, the fewer problems you will run into down the road. Some of the questions you ask may yield information you want to hear. But you should keep in mind that some of the answers may cause unrest. Still, all will be helpful. Even when you uncover that your man has certain problems, you will be able to make healthier choices about whether he is the right man for you.

Christ Waits for Us

Woven throughout the Scriptures we see pictures of the heart of God; a God who waits for us to commit ourselves to Him. We see a patient Lord with His disciples—though they disappointed Him time and again, He waited for them. Though they could not keep watch in His time of prayer in the Garden, they were still His friends. Though He wanted to believe Peter's dedication to Him, and certainly knew he would lead His church, He waited for him to be ready.

We read consistently in the Scriptures about His grief for the city of Jerusalem. Perhaps the most well-known Scripture is found in the gospel of Luke.

> O Jerusalem, Jerusalem, you who kill the prophets and stone those sent to you, how often I have longed to gather your children together, as a hen gathers her chicks under her wings, but you were not willing! Look, your house is left to you desolate. I tell you, you will not see me again until you say, "Blessed is he who comes in the name of the Lord" (Luke 13:33-34).

Later in the New Testament we read of John's vision, when all things are restored, when healing flows freely and dissension is over. The Lord's patience is complete. Listen to John's passion:

> Then I saw a new heaven and a new earth, for the first heaven and the first earth had passed away, and there was no longer any sea. I saw the Holy City, the new Jerusalem, coming down out of heaven from God, prepared as a bride beautifully dressed for her husband. And I heard a loud voice from the throne saying, "Now

the dwelling of God is with men, and he will live with them. They will be his people, and God himself will be with them and be their God. He will wipe every tear from their eyes. There will be no more death, or mourning or crying or pain, for the old order of things has passed away" (Revelation 21:1-4).

Accepting the Scepter

Almost hidden in the pages of Scripture is the small book of Esther. It tells the story of a young girl named Hadassah, orphaned as a child and raised by her cousin Mordecai. Hadassah certainly must have felt abandoned at times. I'm sure she wondered what would become of her life. But, thankfully, God isn't limited by who we are now or the mess we have made of things in the past. He looks at our authentic self and the potential of who we can be. And God saw something incredible in this orphan girl.

Hadassah became a beautiful young woman, but even her beauty betrayed her as the king commanded her to join his harem. What she didn't know was that God was using this situation as a divine appointment in which she would be a candidate to become queen. Through very unusual circumstances, Hadassah rises from her modest means and is selected by King Ahasuerus to accept the scepter, a symbol of dominion and governance, and become Queen Esther. Her rise to power is miraculous, but we also see in her a sense of determination and belief in herself and her mission. She is focused and sure of what she must do. She goes on to deliver her Jewish people from bondage.

It is now your turn to consider how you might rise to royalty, how you might accept the scepter of dominion and authority. During your quest for a committed relationship, you must first discover and fully realize your royal status as a child of God. Remember your status: "You are a chosen people, a royal priesthood, a holy nation, a people belonging to God" (1 Peter 2:9). Once you fully understand that, you will settle for nothing less than a relationship with a man willing and able to commit himself to you emotionally, physically, and spiritually.

My hope is that you are now ready to consider the next stage of commitment: getting your prince ready for commitment.

Let's see how this might be done.

TEN

PREPARING THE PRINCE

I dwell in Possibility.

EMILY DICKINSON

Snips and snails and puppy-dog tails;
That's what little boys are made of.

ANONYMOUS

I have had the privilege of watching a prince prepare himself for his princess. Not literally, mind you. But it was close enough for me.

On June 11, 2005, I watched my oldest son, Joshua, offer himself—chaste, moral, and fully committed—to his princess. It was one of those real-life magical moments when all things are just as they should be.

Now, before you dismiss this as nothing more than a story told by an overly sentimental father gushing about his son and his bride, consider the possibility that Joshua actually was like a prince and his bride like a princess. Can such wonderful, heart-gripping love stories still happen? I'm here to testify that dreams can come true.

The wedding was a majestic and regal affair. As the cars pulled up outside the church, I greeted friends and family dressed in their finery. I was King for a Day, greeting the guests while they wished me well and offered compliments for the handsome couple.

Then came the processional, which offered a hint of anticipation for the wedding ceremony. Well-wishers exchanged quiet whispers and teary-eyed glances. The organ played, the wedding party was escorted to the altar—the place of honor and future sacrifice—and the ceremony began. Candles were lit; songs were sung. The "royal couple" exchanged solemn and sacred vows. It was a most holy ritual.

But the best was yet to come.

After the wedding ceremony, the crowd gathered to offer respect and good wishes. Joshua sat at a table with Jacqueline, his younger brother, and her two younger sisters. In a surprising gesture, amidst raucous laughter and gaiety, Joshua grabbed the microphone and burst into spontaneous speech. A hush fell over the crowd as he looked lovingly at his new bride and exclaimed:

"Jacqueline, this is the happiest moment of my life. I have waited for this day for years. I have been preparing myself for you. You make me a better person. You make me want to try harder in everything I do. You make me want to be a strong person, a devout and loving husband, a faithful companion. I am fully committed to you and love you from the bottom of my heart. I will love you forever."

The crowd was silent. We watched as their eyes met, as Joshua kissed Jacqueline softly on the forehead.

Here was the story of Cinderella, only this time in real life. A young man finds the delight of his life, and she is a princess. She finds the man of her dreams, and he is a prince.

As I watched the scene unfold, I let the images we had seen earlier float through my mind. We had watched a slide show of the pair as children, the images telling the story of how Jacqueline had come to be a beautiful woman. We watched Joshua navigate through awkward years to become the graceful prince he is today.

With tears in my eyes, I was lost in a world of memories as I recalled the years of experiences that had led to this magical moment. It took incredible restraint for me not to jump up and say, "Yes! This is my son. He was once a rebellious and challenging child, but he has become a prince. Please give him all the respect and honor a prince deserves."

Imagine a young man, a boy actually, who drove cars with reckless abandon, let his pants hang embarrassingly low off his hips, and sported so many body piercings that he looked like he was ready to spring a leak. He flirted with the law and always seemed on the edge of suffering some serious injury. He sat unhappily through many church services and constantly crossed the lines his parents had drawn. He often seemed closer to reform school than to any princely palace.

But things gradually changed—so slowly, in fact, that I hardly noticed. A leavening process took hold, leading up to that wonderful day in June.

Just how had this change come about? What factors contributed to his transformation? I know that part of it was simply the result of maturation, but I am convinced that a strong and stable family life also played a significant role:

- He spent considerable time at the dining room table, sharing meals and fellowship with his parents and brother.
- He participated in family life, family vacations, family discussions, and the resolution of family conflicts.
- He flirted with destructive choices but eventually made healthy decisions.

- He experienced the loving support of his parents, even during times when he was testing and striving for independence.

- He spent years in youth group, not always liking it but at least participating on some level.

- He went on mission trips as a youth and later as a college student.

- He accepted Jesus as his personal Savior and found a strong faith of his own.

- He participated in a Christian college program and went to church regularly as a university student.

- He became a student of the Bible.

- He decided he was going to be a one-woman man, fully committed and faithful to Jacqueline.

While Joshua was growing into a fine young man, Jacqueline was growing into a fine young woman. Having spent some time with her, I discovered that her journey went something like this:

- Jacqueline grew up in a loving family, secure and certain of her skills and abilities.

- She participated in family activities that gave her a sense of confidence.

- She examined destructive choices and recognized that they were not right for her.

- She accepted the Lord as her Savior.

- She discussed her dating life with her sisters and parents and gained a clear understanding of healthy expectations.

- She selected a man who echoed some of her strengths and complemented some of her passions.

- She set her sights on a man of integrity, one who was willing to stand by his convictions.

- She searched for a man who loved the Lord and would use the Bible as a source of direction in his life.

- She insisted on a man who would commit himself fully to her, just as she was willing to commit herself fully to him.

But what does my fairy tale have to do with the larger story contained in this book?

Joshua and Jacqueline's story illustrates that having guiding principles and preparing to create a lasting, committed relationship are key steps in turning dreams into reality.

What else must you consider as you do all that you can to ready your prince for a life of emotional and physical commitment?

Kissing a Lot of Frogs

Now that we have discussed Cinderella and her magical life with the prince, and gotten a glimpse of Joshua and Jacqueline's nearly idyllic new life together, we must return to reality. What if your man is not a prince and in fact seems a lot more like a toad? What can you do?

You can take a number of practical steps. Some of these help reinforce the necessity of setting high standards when seeking a prince.

First, realize that only he can decide to be a committed prince. Even if you make excellent choices, clarify your expectations, and set healthy boundaries, he makes the final decision about whether to enter the school of prince making. He decides if he is willing to grow with you emotionally, physically, and spiritually.

Some men truly are card-carrying commitment-phobes who choose to remain stuck in that condition. When that is the case, you can do nothing to change them. They would still feel hemmed in even if you moved across the country and only called every other leap year. That is their makeup, and it has nothing to do with you. Nothing. These men are troubled—they have unresolved issues from their childhood or from earlier relation-ships, have not done their healing work, and bring that baggage to you—and their burdens are too heavy for you to carry.

Likewise, some men are willing to stay in a marriage or rela-tionship but are unwilling to commit themselves fully. They too are troubled. These men are often emotionally underdeveloped. They have never allowed themselves to be emotionally vulnerable, and you can't do much to get them to that place now. They have likely never felt safe sharing their real selves, and their character is often disturbed. You are unlikely to be able to make them feel safe enough to open up to you. You need to understand that you cannot heal them. You cannot fix them. Only they are capable of doing that.

Second, set a measured pace for the relationship. In *Men Who Can't Love,* Steven Carter warns against getting swept off your feet by a whirlwind romance that may end three weeks later. Carter says that men often feel uncomfortable when a relationship moves too quickly. Also, this rapid pace is not healthy for you. He says, "You won't be missing much by keeping a tight grip on the reins, and you may be gaining everything. If he can't handle your slower pace, it's all the more indication that he's not in this for the long haul."[1]

Recently, I met with a young woman, Bethany, whose new boyfriend, Daniel, was at first very involved and anxious to see her. Bethany was a modestly attractive woman, quite reserved and cautious in her attire and presentation, and very polite. She told me that she was thrilled by his early attention, especially the flowers and cards for the first several weeks. However, as time went by, she noticed that his interest cooled. The cards quit coming, the phone calls grew fewer and further apart, and their time together was stilted.

Apparently, Daniel was willing to date Bethany and share some good times, but his pace was certainly different from hers. Even after three months of dating, she felt as if she hardly knew him. When she made attempts to learn more about him, he either laughed them off or told her he didn't care to talk about personal matters. Bethany enjoyed his company but was picking up strong signals that he either did not have the ability to become emotionally vulnerable or had a different agenda regarding the pace of their relationship.

Bethany explored her feelings in counseling. She explained that she had been in this position before—waiting too long to discuss important dating issues, letting the man determine the pace for the relationship. She decided that she had to change.

I agreed. If she is going to continue the relationship with Daniel, she will need to ask him pointedly whether or not he is "in," as well as discuss the pace of their relationship. If he is, he will need to agree to work together on becoming more intimate emotionally with Bethany at a pace they agree upon. If he fails to agree with this stipulation, she must consider ending the relationship.

Third, show him that you can be independent. Having a healthy interdependent relationship is critical. This means that you have a self separate from him, a life independent of his. You are neither looking to him for your happiness nor allowing him to look to you for his happiness. Too much dependence, on either part, is a sure way to sabotage the relationship.

Later, Bethany told Daniel that she wanted a relationship with him but that he had to be willing to move at the same pace as her. The relationship could not work if she were more intimate emotionally than he. She let him know that she was willing to walk away rather than compromise her values. Her strength and integrity made a positive impact on him.

Fourth, let him know that you are a woman of integrity. Although it may startle him to learn that you are not willing to be intimate with him prior to commitment, he will surely respect you for it. Your expectations that he be emotionally, spiritually, and physically committed may surprise him, but those expectations will also make you a prize. A woman of integrity is hard to find, and he knows it. If he cannot see this, then you can rest assured that he is not your prince.

On that note, Carter discusses the importance of not playing house or getting too close too soon. "If you're not married, don't act as though you are. What does that mean? Simple. Don't let him get into the habit of treating you like a wife while he acts like a sometime guest."[2] Be careful, he advises, not to take care of a man early in the relationship. Although some women may naturally use all of their well-honed skills to make their men feel good, this can establish a very troubling precedent because he can easily begin to take you for granted.

Fifth, take care of yourself. Although this may seem like a trite saying, it is true. We are encouraged in Scripture to love others as we love ourselves. There is no virtue in sacrificing yourself on the altar of half-hearted commitment. If you over-function while he under-functions the relationship is doomed. You will end up feeling resentful, and he will end up feeling uncomfortable as well. Regardless of how the relationship turns out, you must be there for yourself. You must show your mate that you can make it on your own if necessary.

Finally, maintain a healthy relationship with God. God will never disappoint you. God will never abandon you. God will always understand and offer guidance. Following scriptural principles is the surest way to remain healthy, both emotionally and relationally.

A healthy relationship with God involves a healthy relationship with His Word. "For the word of God is living and active. Sharper than any double-edged sword, it penetrates even to dividing soul and spirit, joints and marrow; it judges the thoughts and attitudes of the heart" (Hebrews 4:12).

The Search for Your Prince

Some of you may be snickering when I suggest that finding a prince is not an impossible task. Perhaps you have been waiting for your prince to show up, only to be met at the door by the FedEx man—who is already married—or the Schwan delivery guy—single, but not your type.

I am surprised by the number of women who continue to wait for their prince, believing that God will bring the right man to their door. They have excused themselves from any responsibility in the search and have therefore overlooked many healthy prospects. Does that description fit you? Have you believed that God does the matchmaking, and you simply need to wait for the doorbell to ring and your skin to start tingling?

Another common mistake I see women make is eliminating prospects too quickly. If they don't see stars and hear bells ringing, they assume the man cannot be a possible mate. Remember that looks are only skin deep, but character goes all the way to the bone—and character is what you will be living with long after the lightheadedness disappears.

Some women spend far too much time with toads when they could be conducting a finely honed search for a prince. Finding a prince of a man will be a difficult task, but you must realize that your prince may be right in front of you even if you don't recognize him. Because you may have been kissing a lot of toads, you might not notice a prince even if he steps right up and announces his presence.

Let's review how you will be able to distinguish a prince from a toad. What are the differences?

- A prince comes back around, long after that initial wonderful evening of flowers and dancing. Unlike the toad, he is not scared off by the emotional intensity, the closeness, or the promise of more in the future. He enjoys the warmth and passion involved in making true contact.

- He seeks you out consistently and continually. You are not forced to sit by the phone, waiting for him to call. The prince calls because he wants to see you. The toad, on the other hand, avoids follow-up contact that might suggest he is actually interested in a relationship.

- He asks about you and is genuinely concerned with your well-being. He remembers the things that are important to you. He knows what makes you happy and does what he reasonably can to satisfy you. The toad thinks only of himself and his needs.

- He shares in the responsibilities for making the relationship work. He is, as I am fond of saying, "in the game." He realizes that it takes two to tango, and because he wants to dance, he will help learn the steps. He is willing to work on the problems that inevitably arise. He doesn't run when the going gets tough. He cares enough about you to work at keeping the emotional bridge clear of any emotional debris. The toad would rather ford a raging stream than agree to cross that emotional bridge.

- He wants to grow emotionally, spiritually, and physically with you. He has done some of his own emotional and spiritual work and knows what that looks like. Not only can he take care of himself emotionally, but he is willing, when appropriate, to take care of you as well. He is willing to explore and share spiritual matters together. Not so for the toad, who shies away from divulging anything that might make him seem vulnerable.

- He is faithful. He is a one-woman man. He closes off the other options. You both know that you can opt out at any time, but you have decided together that you want to be exclusive with one another. You want to create a safe place where you can blossom as a couple. The true prince commits while the toad plays around.

Please note that most items on the list above are related to *character—not initial impressions.*

Bridge to the Benefit

In a previous career, Christie worked as an account executive for United Way. Her job was to convince reluctant givers that their hard-earned money should be spent helping needy individuals and organizations. She used a technique that is worth mentioning here, one that can be useful in encouraging your man to commit. It's called the "bridge to the benefit." Let's consider what this might look like in your relationship with the commitment-phobic man.

Jim: "I don't want to give up my independence yet. I don't want to have to tell anyone where I'm going or what I'm doing."

Pamela: "Yes, I know where you're coming from. I recognize the importance of spending time by myself. I like the feeling of independence too. I know that both of us will need our own time and our own friends. I look forward to my independent time as well as our time alone."

Let's try another.

Stan: "I'm not sure I'm able to share my emotions the way you want me to."

Karen: "I hear your concern about your ability to be vulnerable. I'm looking forward to growing with you as we practice sharing our feelings."

And one more for good measure:

Todd: "I've never been committed to just one person before."

Kelly: "I hear your concern that you might be frightened of committing yourself to me, but I also hear that maybe you're ready to give it a try and experience a deeper attachment."

What are the key ingredients in this technique?

- Listen to and acknowledge his concerns.
- Empathize with them.

- Validate his concerns.
- Help him see the benefits of making the move he is already considering.

Each of these examples are ways to see if you can find a prince inside your man. You can illustrate the benefits of commitment, ideas he may not have fully considered.

Expanding the Possibilities

I am indebted to authors Rosamund Stone Zander and Benjamin Zander for their excellent book *The Art of Possibility*. This is one of the most powerful tools I have ever encountered for moving from limited thinking to expansive thinking. Obviously, as you consider encouraging your man to grow into his princely potential, you need to rid yourself of limited, narrow approaches.

The Art of Possibility is all about moving from "me" to "we." It is about creating a mind-set that says, "I am no longer principally concerned only about how I am doing but how we are doing." For the healthy couple, this movement is discernable. It is palpable. The Zanders explain:

> The WE story defines a human being in a specific way: It says we are our central selves seeking to contribute, naturally engaged, forever in a dance with each other. It points to relationship rather than individuals, to communication patterns, gestures, and movement rather than to discrete objects and identities...By telling the WE story, an individual becomes a conduit for this new inclusive entity, wearing its eyes and ears, feeling its heart, thinking its thoughts, inquiring what is best for US.[3]

Although the Zanders use a different tone, their message sounds much like the apostle Paul's:

For by the grace given me, I say to every one of you: Do not think of yourself more highly than you ought, but rather think of yourself with sober judgment, in accordance with the measure of faith God has given you. Just as each of us has one body with many members, and these members do not all have the same function, so in Christ we who are many form one body, and each member belongs to all the others. We have differing gifts, according to the grace given us (Romans 12:3-6).

We live, breathe, and exist in community. Will your man see this? Will he decide that this community of two is more valuable than living in isolation?

Steven and Dana are 25-year-olds who came to see me because they were struggling with the issue of commitment in their marriage. They were bright, attractive, and spirited. Well-educated and professional, they clearly did not need each other, at least not financially. So what was their problem?

"How can I help you?" I asked as the session began.

"To be honest," Steven said, "we're not sure we want to be together anymore. We enjoyed our first year of marriage, but ever since then things just haven't been the same."

"It seems like he does his thing," Dana said, "which is working 12 hours a day, and I do my thing—working my job and running the home. We're married in name, but not in spirit. We love each other, but we are wondering if there is any real reason to stay married."

"Why do you even want to explore that?" I asked. "I thought things weren't working."

"We've been married three years," Steven said. "I think both of us believe that we can still make something of it. It's not too late to work on things. We know we have to give up some of our independence, but maybe it will be worth it."

Dana jumped in at that point.

"We know we have a lot to gain, but we also disagree on a lot of things. We find it easier to just do our own thing rather than fight. I guess we just avoid our hot buttons—money, work, the jobs around the house…I'm not sure how easy it would be to change that."

Steven and Dana had to learn a new way of relating. They had to learn more about what the Zanders call WE thinking. They had to shift from an individual orientation to a couple's perspective.

We spent the balance of that session, and several more following, talking about their marriage and what they would gain by working on it. Commitment has many benefits, and they came to see that in their time with me.

In this arena of WE thinking, you can sense or hear what couples are wondering:

- "How are we going to solve this problem?"
- "What can I do to make you more comfortable in this situation?"
- "I want you to be happy with this decision. What do you need?"

Steven and Dana left my office six weeks later with a new perspective. They made some changes that helped them see and feel the benefit of the committed relationship. They regained a new appreciation for the sacredness of marriage—the value of being a prince and princess for one another.

Patience, Not Naïveté

Perhaps your most intricate and important task in this whole endeavor of seeking a committed relationship, a prince, is practicing patience while not being swallowed up in naïveté. You must be wise in your decisions, keen in your wisdom, steadfast without being belligerent. Preparing your prince is, in large part, acting with conviction toward him. Having certitude without being pushy. Communicating expectations without being controlling. How can you find this balance?

You can begin by keeping your goal squarely in mind. Imagine that you are a marathon runner. You have 26.2 miles to go. Starting out too quickly will tire you far before the finish line.

I distinctly remember my first foray into competitive running. I decided to enter a Year-to-Year 5K race that began at midnight in Longview, Washington. I had decided that I would not only run the race but win my division as well. How tough could it be to maintain a swift pace for a little more than three miles? The others, I told myself, would be running for fun, but I would add a little competitive zip to the field.

And so, with neither training nor wisdom at my disposal, I started the race like a jackrabbit. I bolted out in front of most of the 200 participants. Surely, I said to myself, I had to be leading those in my age group. I could already envision a winner's medal draped around my neck.

Until the two-and-a-half-mile mark, when I started to cramp.

My stomach began doing somersaults, heaving up and down, and my dinner was not far behind. I began seeing stars as I became lightheaded. In my foolish desire to win, I not only became sick but barely managed to finish the race. I have since learned the advantage of pacing oneself.

Likewise, pacing yourself in the process of developing a committed relationship is key. You should not start too fast, but you also should not go too slowly. You want to be patient with your man as you each develop these skills of emotional, spiritual, and physical commitment—but not too patient. You don't want to be foolish in your expectations. If he is willing to work toward a long-term relationship with you, that is a good thing. If not, you need to know as soon as possible.

You never want to be naive in matters of commitment. You may have your head in the clouds, so ask a trusted friend for feedback and be willing to listen to wise counsel.

Listen to the apostle Paul on the subject of pacing:

> Do you not know that in a race all the runners run, but only one gets the prize? Run in such a way as to get the prize. Everyone who competes in the games goes into strict training. They do it to get a crown that will not last; but we do it to get a crown that will last forever (1 Corinthians 9:24-25).

Just as you prepare your man for commitment, Jesus prepared His disciples for true commitment. We read in the gospels that He taught His disciples and the crowds of people what following Him would entail. The gospels are replete with examples of how following Jesus, the true Prince of Peace, required leaving other loyalties behind (Luke 9:56-62). Being a follower of Christ is no small matter and must be considered earnestly. Jesus knew we have divided loyalties, as in the case of the young ruler who did not want to give up his personal wealth to follow Christ (Luke 18:18-24).

Men Need Women

I have come to realize that I need Christie. This insight did not jump out at me but rather developed over time. I entered our relationship with the notion that "we'll see what can happen here." I wanted to be open to possibilities—and the possibilities have been delightful.

As I listened to my heart, I sat for hours, journaling, praying, and reflecting on our relationship. I can see that she is a great companion. But I am not with her because I cannot be alone. I have proven to myself that I am good company. I've simply learned that Christie is better company.

I have been astonished to watch Christie give me the space and time I need to come to the realization that she is the woman I want to be with. Sometimes she pushed a bit too hard, but when we talked things out, she always allowed me time to see my way. At all times, she was willing to let our relationship go, which gave me confidence in her. She did not need me to be happy. She allowed me the freedom to choose her.

Daphne Rose Kingma, in her book *The Men We Never Knew*, provides some wonderful wisdom:

> One of the best kept secrets about men is that men need women so much. Our social mythology, of course, is that women need men so much. Women have to trick and trap men into wanting them, because, so the myth goes, women need men so desperately and men don't need women at all. Women have to be gorgeous, sexy, intelligent, charming, submissive, and irresistible, so they can get a man—the man who, supposedly, can live without them but whom they can't possibly live without.
>
> In this view, men are stalwart, sturdy and strong; they do what they want; they have all the power, all the money, and all the opportunity...But, the truth is that men need women far more than women imagine, and in a much deeper way.

Okay, I suppose I'm blowing men's cover by revealing this information and affording you women lots of power through this knowledge, but you really knew it all along, right? Still, it's an important truth, one that will assist you as you relate to men. It will help you to avoid giving your man so much power. He really needs you. In spite of what he says, and in spite of what he does, he really does need you. Kingma tells us how.

> Men need women to love them, to give their lives meaning, to prove to themselves they're real men, to

give them a place to come home to. Men need women in order to approach their own emotional experience: to recreate the nurturing bond that was broken with their mothers, to grant the withheld blessing from their fathers, to replicate the affection of their sisters, to erase the competition with their brothers.

Men need women to love them so they don't feel abandoned, so they can feel their feelings vicariously, so they can get their emotional needs met without having to express them in words, so they can be connected to the spiritual, so they can feel human. Far from being powerful, omnipotent heroes women fantasize them to be, men are emotionally fragile.[4]

I strongly agree with Kingma that all this talk about men being distant, detached, and coolly indifferent to relationships is, for the most part, nothing but myth. Although we may not know how to say what we need or share it in language that makes sense, we need women.

So, what now? Now you know that some men would walk across hot coals to be in a relationship with you. Some men would give their right arm to be married to you. Some men would swim the English Channel to learn how to relate to you in an emotionally vulnerable way.

If you fail to grasp this, you will probably settle for far too little and continue proffering the myth that all men are John Waynes. You might give yourself away for next to nothing. And you are worth so much.

You are now armed with a powerful secret, one that can give you greater courage and belief in yourself. This will be the most effective way to get your prince ready for commitment—approaching the relationship by understanding that your prince needs you.

So, what about me?

Well, I'm hooked. *I can't stand it.* I can't fake it. I can't pretend to be tough when I am so tender. I'll continue down this path of commitment with Christie. And she's reading every word of this!

How about you? Will you pursue commitment? Will you value yourself enough to demand a committed relationship? Your man really can get there.

EPILOGUE:
CONTINUING THE JOURNEY TO
HEALTHY COMMITMENT

In the evening of life, we will be judged on love alone.

ST. JOHN OF THE CROSS

We have come a long way together in this book. The topic has not been an easy one to deal with, but we have not shied away from the challenges. We must confront things directly if we are to find commitment or demand commitment in our relationships. I sincerely believe that positive change is possible, and I have counseled you to look closely at yourself to consider the choices you have been making. Simply put, healthier choices lead to an improved life and more robust relationships.

In this closing chapter I want to review where we have been and where we still need to go. I will do my best to make sure that both your route and your destination are clearly marked.

In a few short weeks I will embark on a road trip with a clear beginning—Seattle, Washington—and also a clear destination—Yellowstone National Park. I will be accompanying my youngest son, Tyson, on a portion of his journey from Seattle to New York City, where he will attend medical school in the fall.

Last evening Tyson and I sat down and excitedly planned part of our trip. Sitting at the kitchen table with an oversized, earmarked, coffee-stained atlas as our guide, we mapped out some of the stops along the way to Old Faithful, which I have not visited since I was a child. We highlighted areas of interest: friends in Spokane; a national park or two in Idaho and Montana; and then, of course, Yellowstone.

I am inclined to lay out the exact course in advance—mileage, times of travel, special stopovers, where we will spend the night. For me, the best surprise is no surprise at all. That is not the case for Tyson. His backpack contains most of his worldly goods and is his most intimate companion. He likes to wander, watching for opportunities to pursue along the way. His destination is the same as mine—Yellowstone Park—but he prefers a path that is lighter, more gentle than mine might have been.

I am inclined to fuss and fume about every little thing I might need while on the road. My gear includes a flashlight, matches, and AAA's highlighted map. Tyson is content with gasoline in the tank and four tires with decent tread. He is satisfied to trust in his own skills, not becoming too attached to any "right" way of doing things. His style unnerves me, but it also intrigues me. What if I were able to lighten my load? What if I were more inclined to trust myself and the loving hand of God to guide me on my journey—the forthcoming literal one, as well as the ongoing emotional and spiritual one? What if I were less intent on setting the destination and simply took time to look around to see and enjoy things I would otherwise have missed? Can I have a goal, a structure, and yet allow for unforeseen possibilities? To live in the future and yet fully in the moment? That is my goal and one I would recommend for you as well.

I envy Tyson's freedom and self-confidence. He is content to move slowly and deliberately, to really observe the world around him. He spends time reflecting on his life, his relationships, and their meaning to him. During the last two years, he has ambled from one place to another, listening and learning. He has taught me some critical lessons, and although I confess to being a bit out of my comfort zone, I am anxious to travel with him—listening for subtle nuances to guide us, finding unconventional ways to solve routine problems, living in kairos time—time without demands and agendas—making choices I might not otherwise make.

You too are on a journey. You too have an opportunity to travel a bit differently than you did in the past. You have an opportunity to listen to your heart and make choices you might not otherwise have made. You can try something new, take some chances, set your heart free. This final chapter is about taking inventory of your journey, where you are on it, and how you are traveling.

You have chosen this book because you want to be in a relationship with a man who is willing to commit himself fully to you. You want a man who understands that part of intimacy is letting you "into me see." You want a man willing to close the back door, lock it, and throw away the key. But you have picked up this book because what you have been doing is not working for you. Perhaps you have recognized yourself in one or more of the chapters in this book. Perhaps you have been sabotaging yourself, connecting with detached men, fearing commitment, having difficulty identifying princely qualities.

We both know your destination. We simply need to establish a new travel plan that includes holding on to the vision, letting go of rigid control, knowing what you need in a man, and trying out new possibilities.

A journey is more delightful if we can keep these seemingly disparate possibilities in mind at all times. We are then free to experience life and develop new skills. When we rigidly cling to the way we think things ought to be, we simply create more stress (and distress) for ourselves.

How you travel and with whom you travel are important considerations for your journey. How much satisfaction you garner from the trip will depend on whether you travel light and fancy-free or encumbered by rigid thinking. Whether you are able to choose your own path is also an important issue. This is *your* journey, and you need to have the freedom to make choices that are healthy for you, even as you are in relationship.

Joyce Meyer, in her book *Approval Addiction,* talks about breaking free from controlling powers:

> If you are letting someone control your life—intimidate you, manipulate you, and cause you to do what you know in your heart is not right—then you need to break those controlling powers. It is not God's will for us to be controlled by anybody except His Holy Spirit, and even that decision He leaves up to us.[1]

The Beginning

Every journey starts at the same place: the beginning. We start at the beginning, much like players of a board game who set out from the square marked Start.

But I am asking you to do more than acknowledge that you are at the beginning of a journey. I want you to take a moment and assess what this jumping-off place is like for you, to understand that this may actually represent a new start in your life. Here are a few ideas to consider as you assess your unique starting point.

- Am I excited about this journey?
- Do I approach this starting place with some fear and trepidation?

- Am I scared to death to move out of my comfort zone?
- Am I traveling alone, or do I have some companions on the journey?
- Am I clear about where I am going?
- Do I know the mile markers that will guide me along the way?
- What kind of support do I have for the journey?

Perhaps these are easy questions for you to answer. You may have moved swiftly through this book and know exactly what kind of man you want, the things that have been holding you back, and how you will resolve your existing problems. If so, you are well on your way.

Or you may be much less confident. Do your best to be objective. Ask yourself how well things are working for you. Perhaps you have chosen one uncommitted man after another but have virtually no idea why you have made those choices. I hope that after our work together in this book, you are now clearer about those issues and ready to travel through the healing process.

Perhaps you have relied on old, ineffective behavior patterns when reaching out for your prince. For example, you may have unresolved issues from your past. Maybe a residue of pain resulting from rejection in your life has created a barrier between yourself and any eligible man. Or perhaps you are in a relationship but have hidden behind busyness or other forms of distancing yourself as a way to avoid intimacy. Maybe you withdraw in response to a man who is distant and detached himself. Regardless of your scenario, I am guessing that you would love to experience a higher level of closeness and caring.

Each story is different. Each life has its own history. Each path to healing must be unique. What is important is that you acknowledge exactly where you are today, celebrate who you are and where you have traveled, and spend time trying to identify and understand the barriers standing between you and an emotionally and physically committed relationship. It is available to you, but as I mentioned previously, don't expect the FedEx man or the Schwan's driver to show up at your door to rescue you. You will need to take action. You will need to map out your journey, allowing for a detour or two, and pursue your destination relentlessly and courageously.

Regardless of where you are, something is always grand about beginnings. Every journey holds the promise of wonder. Like peering out at night on a brilliantly lit city from the tenth floor of a hotel room, you can't help but wonder what is going on out there.

Can you let your imagination take flight? Can you envision something bigger and better than what you currently have?

Your Destination

Having clarified your starting place and honored the path you have taken thus far in your life, you must also identify your destination. As silly as this may sound, many people are as vague about where they are going as where they are starting. Specifically, many are not clear about the kind of man they want. They are not clear about the qualities they want in a relationship. Likewise, they do not know what they are doing that contributes to their problems. With this type of confusion, we should not be surprised that they never reach their destination. Either they are not reading a map that is right for their particular journey, or they have charted the wrong destination.

So, what is your destination, and what are you taking along on your journey? Let me remind you of several things that may help you prepare.

First, remember that you are the one who is responsible for your journey. If you get lost or sidetracked, you can fix your poor planning or miscalculation. You may be tempted, as am I, to blame problems on someone else, but you are the one who is ultimately responsible. If you get lost, ask yourself why this is happening. What must you learn from the experience in order to be able to make meaningful changes in your life?

Second, remember that because you alone are responsible, you can change your journey at any time. Life and God both offer us many opportunities to change our direction. When we are lost, God always offers us a way back to the main road. But we need to be willing to listen to His instructions.

I am reminded of a man who headed into the wilderness on an afternoon trek. He had prepared thoroughly and even used a compass to set his bearings. He decided to hike off the well-marked trail, and after a time, he became disoriented. He leaned heavily on his compass for guidance but found that it seemed to lead him farther from what he surmised was his path home. Finally, he abandoned his compass readings and used his Boy Scout survival training to find his way. After locating the trail, as he was considering his plight, he realized that his compass had been five degrees off course—a minimal error in most circumstances, but enough to get him lost in the woods. For all of us, even a small miscalculation can make a huge difference when we are trying to find our way.

Third, assess where your man is on his own journey. If he is unwilling to work on the relationship and unwilling to commit himself to you, that is important information for setting a course. Is he simply lacking in skills but willing to learn? Does he not understand the severity of the situation? Ultimately, you will also need to ask yourself what can realistically be changed. And, most importantly, you will need to decide if what you are receiving from him is enough for you.

Fourth, remember that you cannot change your man, but you can stop enabling his dysfunctional behavior. Acknowledging that he is distant and emotionally detached is one thing; standing by and doing nothing is quite another. Have you confronted him about his troublesome behavior, or are you tiptoeing around him? Are you identifying areas that need to be changed? Are you insisting on things you need in order to enjoy a mutually beneficial relationship?

Fifth, are you pacing yourself on this journey? We have talked about the importance of not moving too quickly or too slowly. We have talked about the dangers of pushing him so hard that you are effectively sabotaging the relationship. We have also talked about the foolishness of waiting forever for something that is not likely to come. Balance is the key.

Sixth, remember that you must make yourself a princess, readying yourself for your prince. You will wait for your prince forever if you have not worked on your own issues and made yourself ready for life in the kingdom.

Finally, remember that you can do some things to ready your prince. You can help your man see what emotional vulnerability looks like. You can demonstrate to him that you will settle for nothing less than a lasting, committed relationship. You can let him know that you expect emotional honesty and that anything less is unsatisfactory.

These mile markers can help you stay the course to your destination. But more is required. You will need a strong dose of inspiration to reach your goal. Inspiration, along with a lot of faith, will be a primary impetus for keeping your eyes on the prize.

Four Values for Maintaining Inspiration

Dr. Neil Clark Warren, preeminent author and psychologist, writes in his book *Catching the Rhythm of Love* that four values can help you maintain the inspiration you need to stay the course.

Persistence. People achieve greatness because they refuse to give up. Warren tells about Winston Churchill, who took three years to get through the eighth grade because he had trouble learning English grammar. At one point, he was last in his class, and his father gave up on him. But history sees Churchill as a great man regardless of what transpired in the eighth grade.

Many women are discouraged in their search for love. They are ready to throw in the towel even though staying the course can win them the prize. Giving up is not the answer. Persistence pays off.

Courage. A search for a prince is not for the weak at heart. You must believe that your goal is a worthy one. You must have faith in your direction. You must have confidence in your abilities and your mission.

The enemy of courage, of course, is discouragement. Nothing is quite so deflating as discouragement, fueled by your own long-standing doubts. It tells us lies like these:

- There is no hope.
- There are no princes out there.
- Even if there were, you could not win one.
- Maybe you are better off alone.

Don't believe that twisted thinking. Remind yourself, again and again, of the truth:

- There is hope.
- There are princes out there.
- You must continue to be selective in your search.
- You are worthy of being in a relationship with a prince.
- You deserve a healthy, committed relationship.

Generosity. People have said that whatever you give will come back to you. The Scriptures say, "Do to others as you would have them do to you" (Luke 6:31). The point is this: Be generous in your dealings with the world. Do not be foolish with your treasures, but be generous with them. Be a good steward of what God has given to you, and you will be rewarded.

Idealism. Solomon, the author of Ecclesiastes, said it best—"He has made everything beautiful in its time. He has also set eternity in the hearts of men; yet they cannot fathom what God has done from beginning to end" (Ecclesiastes 3:11).

You must press on because God has set eternity in your heart. God said that it was not good for man or woman to be alone. He established relationships and fashioned us for intimacy. You are on solid ground when you seek intimacy and commitment.

Again, discouragement can douse the flames of idealism, but it can never extinguish the fire. Something in each heart continues to long for that special someone. You must press on, for this is how you have been designed.

Warren says, "There is something deep within most human beings that makes us want to reach for our ideals. We yearn to be the best we can be, even when no one else knows how hard we try at any given time. And we like to see others reach for high ideals in their lives too."[2]

Roadblocks

As you consider your path, ask yourself if you have you taken the time to ensure that you are taking full responsibility for it. Have you claimed your path as your own? Are you the one who has fully chosen it, or are you being unduly influenced by others in your life, perhaps from your past? Are you being unduly influenced by someone today, perhaps a man in your life, who is trying to control you and stifle your true voice? Relinquishing control of your life will not help you on your journey. It will only distract you. Let's spend a little time considering some roadblocks you must avoid if you are to safely reach your destination.

Losing Sight of Your Destination. Obviously, if you lose sight of your destination, if you do not keep your goals clearly in mind, you may never arrive. You stand the risk of meandering in the wilderness for a long time, frustrated and discouraged. Keep your focus on the destination, and your chances of reaching it will increase dramatically.

Losing Sight of the Path. While pursuing our goals, we must also keep moving forward, one step at a time. We must be patient with the obstacles that will inevitably obstruct us and find ways to navigate around them. In fact, sometimes we may need to take an alternate route. Just because things don't work out on one path does not mean we have to give up on the goal.

Losing Your True Voice. Many voices in your life will be eager to tell you how you ought to proceed. Be careful. Not all of those voices will be supportive of you. You must learn to discern a helpful voice from one that will take you off course.

Losing Sight of Your Strengths. Someone once said that if you have survived childhood, you have a story worth celebrating. I believe that is true. Even if you hate some things about your past, within that distress lie the courage and hope that are the seeds of change. Each life is an incredible work of the Creator and is worth championing.

Losing Sight of Your Safety. Even as you attempt to improve the quality of your relationship, you must always remember to be a good steward of your life, your self, your soul. As Julia Cameron says in her book *The Sound of Paper,* "As prissy as it may sound, 'Be careful' is useful creative advice. It means to be gently thoughtful of yourself and your progress, not to expect too much or, on the other hand, to require too little."[3] Once again, the key is balance—moving forward while also being sensitive to your safety and well-being.

Losing Your Faith. Your faith, your relationship to God, is the strength you need to continue the journey. If you don't believe that God is behind every step you take, you will succumb to self-doubt. Remember this: "But the counselor, the Holy Spirit, whom the Father will send in my name, will teach you all things and will remind you of everything I have said to you" (John 14:26).

Not long ago, a 50-year-old woman named Jenny came to see me. I noticed her fidgeting in my waiting room, her face pinched and taut, her eyes darting back and forth from one object to another. She was dressed modestly in slacks and blouse, and her graying hair was slightly unkempt. As I observed her for a moment, I imagined her as a wound coil ready to spring.

She did not settle down when she came into my office. She seemed preoccupied, distracted. I asked her to share her story, but she told me she was not sure why she had come.

After I'd asked a few questions and helped her to relax, Jenny told me that she was profoundly discouraged in her search for a committed man. She spoke slowly and deliberately, as though she were not really certain about her feelings. Her discouragement settled like heavy air in the room. She shared the following story.

"I was divorced several years ago from an abusive man. He was controlling and mean-tempered, and after 25 years of marriage I called it quits. I felt terrible about divorcing because I know what God thinks of divorce. Maybe what happened was my fault. I don't know. But I didn't feel like He wanted me to stay with an abusive man. I have been single for several years. It took me years to start dating. I just wanted to go to work and keep to myself. When I finally did start to date, I didn't have a positive experience. I just couldn't seem to find any good men out there. I decided being alone was better than compromising my values."

"Tell me about your dating process," I said.

"There's not much to tell. I got involved in a singles' program at a local church and went on a few dates, but I felt like the guys there were just as worldly as the ones I met at work."

"How many dates have you had since your divorce, Jenny?"

"A few. None of them good. Now I guess I'm turned off. I've gone to some singles meetings and some outings sponsored by the church. But being around some of those guys was enough for me."

Jenny and I talked for several months about her troubled marriage, her painful divorce, and her disappointing experience with men at the singles program. We discussed how Jenny seemed to be sidetracked from her goal, which, I discovered, was very unclear. Her life seemed to epitomize many of the detours women make in pursuit of their goals. She had lost her destination, her path, her voice, and much of her faith.

- She did not have a clear goal in mind regarding dating.
- She did not believe in herself or her ability to attract a good man.
- She did not listen to herself but believed others who discouraged her about the chances of finding a good man.
- She did not practice effective strategies that would help her reach her goal.
- She did not have a clear faith to support her journey.
- She did not act like a princess, readying herself for her prince.

Jenny warmed up in counseling. In fact, I learned that she is a very likeable woman who simply did not believe in herself. She had never taken the time to honor her journey—detours and all—and no one was encouraging her to move forward toward a fulfilling destination.

Jenny had her work cut out for her, but within six months she was dating—and this time with more enjoyment. She became clearer about the kind of man she wanted to date, made herself available to opportunities, and made her expectations clear to her dates. She narrowed her target to men with strong character, and she enjoyed her journey. She spent time grieving her past, celebrating her strengths, and slowly regaining her confidence. She now has the hope of finding a successful relationship with a healthy man, one who is committed to her.

No Commitment, No Love

Although this book is written primarily for women who are hoping to find commitment in their love lives, men should read it as well. Both women and men need to understand the paramount importance of commitment in relationship, and the responsibility to make this happen does not rest on women alone.

Without commitment, love is shallow. In relationships—and nowhere else—we are challenged to really love another person. In relationships we let our vulnerabilities and personality issues show.

Loving from a distance is easy. I am an expert at that. I look back on my life and realize that many of my personal failures have been the result of profound selfishness—failing to really reach outside myself to give to others sacrificially.

If Scott Peck is right when he says, in *The Road Less Traveled*, that love means extending yourself—really stretching out—for the welfare of others, then I have been, in some ways, a colossal failure. Too often I have loved from a distance. Maybe you can relate.

I like to love as long as I stand little risk of being hurt in return. I like to give just to the point where it begins to hurt, and then back off. I seem to have some innate mechanism that is like a yellow light warning me that I am about to be called upon to give too much, to the point where it might hurt a bit. Perhaps I speak for a lot of men when I ask, "Can't I love without having to give so much?" The answer is a resounding *no!*

I cannot gloss over my failed marriage. Let's just say that I will do many things differently in my new relationship—and loving sacrificially, in a fully committed way, is at the top of the list. Most men share my sentiments. We wonder about our abilities to relate to women at all. The bottom line is this: We must work on being fully committed—emotionally and physically.

Why have I emphasized that this issue of commitment is so important? Because only *in the safety of a fully committed relationship* can love really blossom. In the safety of being listened to, affirmed, complimented, and assured that the relationship is safe from any forces that might cause it to disintegrate, love flourishes. Although we are quick to say that love is what women need, men really need the same thing. We need to know that whatever happens, regardless of how distressing the conflict was yesterday, the relationship will be safe and intact tomorrow.

In the shelter of this enduring relationship, love will not just abide—it will grow. I am reminded of the tenets offered by famed family therapist Virginia Satir. She suggested, and I agree, that in the comfort of a safe, committed relationship, couples can offer one another the five freedoms. Consider how your relationship fares on each of these:

- the freedom to see and hear what they see and hear, rather than what they are expected to see and hear
- the freedom to think what they think, rather than what they are expected to think
- the freedom to feel what they feel, rather than what they are expected to feel
- the freedom to want what they want, rather than what they are expected to want
- the freedom to imagine what they imagine, rather than what they are expected to imagine

As you move forward on your journey, these five freedoms can serve as mile markers. A healthy relationship features these freedoms. Anyone fully committed to you must also be committed to these principles, for these tenets are what make you who you are. Any man who is truly committed to you knows that you are unique, distinct, and separate from him.

Dropping Your Guard

As long as we avoid this sticky thing called commitment, we never have to be real. And, as the *Velveteen Rabbit* so aptly put it, being real can be painful. Our buttons are likely to get worn off, and we are likely to get hurt. Why else would we isolate ourselves, avoiding the wonderful elements that can be ours by making real contact? Why else would we avoid that incredible feeling of having someone who knows our deepest pain, our worst fear, our most troubling attribute or action, and loves us anyway?

Chuck Swindoll, in his bestselling book *Dropping Your Guard,* tells of years of walking around pretending to be someone he was not. He played the distance game:

> Distance that makes you out of focus with me—removed from me by closed-off compartments that stay locked, keeping us from being able to know each other and, when and where necessary, to help each other…All the uncertainty not withstanding, the rewards of dropping your guard will far outweigh the risks involved…
>
> The purpose of the journey, of course, is not simply to unmask and parade ourselves as we expose the truth of who we are. That's merely a means to an end. The *ultimate* objective is to cultivate an atmosphere of such openness that we are free to share our dreams in an unguarded manner, talk about our hopes, and hammer out our goals in life. By becoming people who are comfortable to be around, we encourage the same in others. In the process, a grinding existence changes into meaningful living as we replace our isolationism with involvement in the lives of others.[4]

And so, in spite of what your man chooses to do, you can address the task of learning when, where, and how to become more vulnerable yourself. You can learn the importance of being real with yourself and selected others. This will stand you in good stead as you move toward expecting those same qualities from the man in your life.

Christ's Commitment to Us

Now we come full circle. We must remind ourselves why we feel the need to talk about this thing called commitment, and why in the world we have such trouble with it.

We are talking about it, of course, because it is a foundational aspect of love. We have trouble with it because ever since the Garden, our critical failure has led to rampant selfishness, irresponsibility, and pride, all of which are antithetical qualities to love and commitment. From the beginning, we have been looking out for number one. We have struggled to get outside of ourselves and tend to the nourishment of others.

But thankfully, we have an example of the way life can be. In Christ we have a model of one who is fully human, fully God, and fully committed to the Father and to us. Consider Christ:

> Who, being in very nature of God, did not consider equality with God something to be grasped, but made himself nothing, taking the very nature of a servant, being made in human likeness. And being found in appearance as a man, he humbled himself and became obedient to death—even death on a cross! Therefore God exalted him to the highest place and gave him the name that is above every name, that at the name of Jesus every knee should bow, in heaven and on earth and under the earth, and every tongue confess that Jesus Christ is Lord, to the glory of God the Father (Philippians 2:6-11).

The apostle Paul beautifully supplements this passage a few verses later. As we come to a close on our short journey together, and as you consider what lies ahead, can you place yourself in these verses and claim the promise as your own?

"Not that I have already obtained all this, or have already been made perfect, but I press on to take hold of all that for which Christ Jesus took hold of me" (Philippians 3:12).

Can you feel the Lord's grasp on your life? Can you feel His commitment to you? This is the type of commitment we must strive for in our relationships.

Writing Him into Your Future

You have reached the end of this book, but I am confident that you will continue on your journey to healthy commitment. Please remember that healthy commitment means being willing to write your man into your future—into every aspect of your life. It is risky business but well worth the effort. If you are currently with a man, then you know some of the steps that you need to take. If you don't have a man in your life at present, you are now aware of some strategies that you can use to prepare yourself for that opportunity.

You may find yourself discouraged by the challenges before you. You may still be uncertain of what lies ahead. That's okay. What matters is that you have begun addressing the issues facing a person who loves another who cannot or will not commit. You have considered why this might be occurring. You have made an earnest effort to understand and unravel the mysteries of love and commitment.

Although I cannot walk in your shoes or fully understand your struggle, I hope that I have at least raised some helpful questions. I trust that you are a deeper person with greater possibilities than you were when we began our journey together.

And I will hope for one more thing. I will hope you will be able to look in the mirror and say, "It is enough that I am taking it one step at a time. It is enough that I know more than I knew a few days or a few weeks ago. It is enough that I trust myself and God to figure things out."

God bless you in your ongoing journey to the fullness and richness of a committed relationship—with Jesus as your constant companion and with high hopes for that wonderful man who will become a part of your life.

NOTES

Prologue: A Healing Journey to Healthy Commitment

1. Paul Reiser, *Couplehood* (New York: Bantam Books, 1994), 151.

2. Scott Peck, *The Road Less Traveled* (New York: Simon and Schuster, 1978), 140-141.

3. Margery Williams, *The Velveteen Rabbit* (New York: Delacorte Press, 1922), 5-8.

4. Eileen Silvia Kindig, *Goodbye Prince Charming* (Colorado Springs: NavPress, 1993), 29.

5. Dean Ornish, *Love and Survival* (New York: HarperCollins Publishers, 1998), 141.

6. Ibid., 143.

Chapter 1—Living What He's Learned

1. Laura Schlessinger, *Ten Stupid Things Women Do to Mess Up Their Lives* (New York: Villard Books, 1994), 113.

2. Sam Keen, *To Love and Be Loved* (New York: Bantam Books, 1997), 175.

3. Ibid., 176.

4. Ibid., 177.

Chapter 2—Falling Short of Great Expectations

1. Pia Melody, *Facing Codependence* (San Francisco: HarperSanFrancisco, 1989), 48-49.

2. Scott Peck, *The Road Less Traveled* (New York: Simon and Schuster, 1978), 141.

3. Dean Ornish, *Love and Survival* (New York: HarperCollins Publishers, 1998), 38.

4. *The New John Gill Exposition of the Entire Bible*. www.searchgodsword.org.

5. Daphne Rose Kingma, *The Book of Love* (Berkeley: Conari Press, 2001), 15.

6. George Weinberg, *Why Men Won't Commit* (New York: Atria Books, 2002), 16.

7. Ibid., 23.

Chapter 3—Come Close, Get Away

1. Mary Ellen Donovan and William Ryan, *Love Blocks* (New York: Viking Press, 1989), 241.

2. Adapted from Jerome Murray, "Are You Growing Up, or Just Getting Older?" www.betteryou.com/maturity.htm.

3. Henri Nouwen, *The Inner Voice of Love* (New York: Inner Books, 1996), 45.

Chapter 4—Sabotaging Relationships

1. Adapted from John Gray, "Are You Sabotaging Your Chances of Finding Love?" www.msn.match.com/msn/article.aspx?articleid=2120&TrackingID=516311&BannerID=544659&GT1=3142.

2. This and other articles by Bryan Redfield are available through his website, www.theredfieldsystem.com.

Chapter 5—Not Ready for Prime Time

1. Mark Nepo, *The Book of Awakening* (Berkeley: Conari Press, 2000), 165.

2. Harville Hendrix, *Keeping the Love You Find* (New York: Atria Books, 1992), 7.

3. Ibid.

4. Ibid., 8.

5. Henri Nouwen, *The Inner Voice of Love* (New York: Inner Books, 1996), 40.

Chapter 6—Yellow Warning Lights

1. Princeton Language Institute, *21st Century Dictionary of Quotations* (New York: Dell Publishing, 1993), 66.

2. Steven Carter and Julia Sokol, *He's Scared, She's Scared* (New York: Dell Publishing, 1993), 59.

3. Barry Lubetkin and Elena Oumano, *Bailing Out* (New York: Fireside, 1993), 77.

Chapter 7—The Real Nature of Commitment

1. Judith Viorst, *Grown-Up Marriage* (New York: The Free Press, 2003), 11.

2. Linda Waite and Maggie Gallagher, *The Case for Marriage* (New York: Doubleday), n.p.

3. John Powell, *Why Am I Afraid to Tell You Who I Am?* (Chicago: Argus Communications, 1969).

4. Ibid., 55.

5. Ibid., 62.

6. Margaret Guenther, *Holy Listening* (Cambridge: Cowley Publications, 1992), 143.

7. Douglas Weiss, *Intimacy* (Lake Mary, FL: Strang Communications Company, 2001), 157.

8. Ibid., 167.

Chapter 8—Commitment Isn't on the Sales Rack

1. Wendy Murray Zoba, "CT Classic: Bonhoeffer in Love," *Christianity Today*, February 12, 2001. Available online at www.christianitytoday.com/ct/2001/107/33.0.html.

2. Laura Schlessinger, *Ten Stupid Things Women Do to Mess Up Their Lives* (New York: Villard Books, 1994), 197.

3. Ibid., 200.

4. Charles Neider, ed., *The Complete Short Stories of Mark Twain* (New York: Doubleday, 1957), 153.

5. Aaron Beck, *Love Is Never Enough* (New York: Harper Paperbacks, 1989), 217.

Chapter 9—When the Princess Is Ready, the Prince Will Appear

1. Marsha Sinetar, *Ordinary People as Monks and Mystics* (Mahwah, NJ: 1986), n.p.

2. Christina Baldwin, *Life's Companion* (New York: Bantam Books, 1991), 257.

3. Ibid., 259.

4. John Welwood, *Journey of the Heart* (New York: HarperCollins Publishers, 1990), 89.

5. Ibid., 90.

Chapter 10—Preparing the Prince

1. Steven Carter, *Men Who Can't Love* (New York: M. Evans and Company, 1987), 224.

2. Ibid., 225.

3. Rosamund Stone Zander and Benjamin Zander, *The Art of Possibility* (Boston: Harvard Business School Press, 2000), 84.

4. Daphne Rose Kingma, *The Men We Never Knew* (Berkeley: Conari Press, 1994), 154.

Epilogue—Continuing the Journey to Healthy Commitment

1. Joyce Meyer, *Approval Addiction* (New York: Warner Books, 2005), 207.

2. Neil Clark Warren, *Catching the Rhythm of Love* (Nashville: Thomas Nelson Publishers, 2000), 115-18.

3. Julia Cameron, *The Sound of Paper* (New York: Jeremy P. Tarcher, 2004), 126.

4. Chuck Swindoll, *Dropping Your Guard* (Dallas: Word Publishing, 1983), 10-11.

Dr. Hawkins is interested in hearing about your journey and may be contacted through his website at www.YourRelationshipDoctor.com

Also by David Hawkins

WHEN PLEASING OTHERS IS HURTING YOU

As a servant of Christ, when you begin to forfeit your own God-given calling and identity in an unhealthy desire to please others, you move from servanthood to codependency. This helpful guide can get you back on track.

DOES YOUR MAN HAVE THE BLUES?

Dr. Hawkins exposes the problem of male depression with unusual compassion and clarity. He describes the telltale signs, pinpoints some of the causes, and suggests ways you can help your man.

SAYING IT SO HE'LL LISTEN

Dr. Hawkins offers straightforward, intelligent counsel for dealing with sensitive topics in a relationship. Readers will find new motivation to press through to the goal of effective communication: reconciliation and greater intimacy in marriage.

NINE CRITICAL MISTAKES MOST COUPLES MAKE

Dr. Hawkins shows that complex relational problems usually spring from nine destructive habits couples fall into, and he offers practical suggestions for changing the way husbands and wives relate to each other.

WHEN TRYING TO CHANGE HIM IS HURTING YOU

Dr. Hawkins offers practical suggestions for women who want to improve the quality of their relationships by helping the men in their lives become healthier and more fun to live with.

HARVEST HOUSE
PUBLISHERS